KU-739-028

THE TAXMAN

THE TAXMAN

BRIAN COCKERILL
WITH
STEPHEN RICHARDS

JOHN BLAKE

Published by John Blake Publishing Ltd,
3 Bramber Court, 2 Bramber Road,
London W14 9PB, England

www.johnblakepublishing.co.uk

First published in paperback in 2007

ISBN: 978 1 84454 488 2

All rights reserved. No part of this publication may be reproduced, stored in a
retrieval system, or in any form or by any means, without the prior permission in
writing of the publisher, nor be otherwise circulated in any form of binding or
cover other than that in which it is published and without a similar condition
including this condition being imposed on the subsequent publisher.

British Library Cataloguing-in-Publication Data:

A catalogue record for this book is available from the British Library.

Design by www.envydesign.co.uk

Printed in Great Britain by CPI Bookmarque, Croydon, CR0 4TD

5 7 9 10 8 6

© Text copyright Brian Cockerill and Stephen Richards

Papers used by John Blake Publishing are natural, recyclable products made from
wood grown in sustainable forests. The manufacturing processes conform to the
environmental regulations of the country of origin.

Every attempt has been made to contact the relevant copyright-holders, but some were
unobtainable. We would be grateful if the appropriate people could contact us.

For my wife Amanda, my son Jordan and my sister Kath
Thank you for looking after me.

Other titles by Stephen Richards

Viv Graham
by Stephen Richards

Insanity: My Mad Life
by Charles Bronson with Stephen Richards

The Krays and Me
by Charles Bronson with Stephen Richards

The Good Prison Guide
by Charles Bronson with Stephen Richards

The Lost Girl
by Caroline Roberts with Stephen Richards

It's Criminal
by Stephen Richards

Born to Fight
by Richy Horsley with Stephen Richards

Street Warrior
by Malcolm Price with Stephen Richards

Crash 'n' Carry
by Stephen Richards

The Taxman
by Brian Cockerill with Stephen Richards

Lost in Care
by Jimmy Holland with Stephen Richards

CONTENTS

INTRODUCTION

Tax = Make heavy demands on someone's powers or resources
Man = An adult human male

Tax Man = Brian Cockerill

Drug = Chemical substance taken for the effect it produces
Dealer = A person or business that buys and sells goods

Drug dealer = A person about to receive a visit from the Tax Man

BRITAIN'S AUTHORITIES HAVE behaved like gangsters for centuries, yet their crimes are always swept under the carpet. The UK is drowning in a sea of illegal drugs, more so than at any time known to man, including me ... the Tax Man! Most crime stems from its birthplace of the murky world of drugs: smackheads and crackheads waiting near post offices to mug old ladies for a few pounds from their handbags, and intent on turning over other vulnerable members of the community for whatever else they can get. All this just so they can get their £5 fix!

I can't do anything about every single junkie that blights their community in the UK, as I'm only one man. However, blitzing the source of the street urchins' drug supply means the drug dealer gets it!

Forget about these academics, community groups and government organisations – they do nothing to help eradicate drug users, or to help the parents. There are thousands of organisations throughout the world whose sole aim is to cut down drug use, all in receipt of big money.

Let's face it, drugs are here to stay – legal and illegal. The tax revenue from legal drugs has brought billions of pounds into the coffers of the bloodsucking British government. Look at the ways we're all taxed from the cradle to the grave and then tell me if that isn't the truth about this mob of Westminster gangsters. They're leeches that cream off our hard-earned cash.

What's the difference between the government and a gangster? A gangster gives you a choice, whereas the government don't! Look at it this way: a gangster will tax business for protection money. The nightclub boss pays a few grand a week for the services of the local muscle. Any trouble that flares is quelled and the troublemakers are hunted down, one by one. Now, if the nightclub boss phones the police, they might turn up, but there's no guarantee they'll get the matter resolved. And, when you consider how much the club boss has forked out to the local council in taxes, he gets fuck all for his money!

You've got no choice but to pay your taxes. Rather than look at what is taxed, look at what isn't taxed: children's clothes and books. At least when you face a vampire, you know you'll be sucked dry of your blood. With government taxation, it doesn't stop there: they chase you for death duties when you're dead and gone!

Pensioners going into care homes have their life savings eaten away by mandatory charges levied against them by the government, and perhaps have had to sell their home, leaving nothing for them to pass on to their families. They've been taxed of the hard-earned dosh that they have worked a lifetime to accrue. Who's the thief that took it away from them? And we allow it to happen!

Just to watch TV you need a licence. Those caught watching the telly without one are paraded before the court, fined up to £1,000 and then shamed and ridiculed by seeing their names appear in the local paper. Should you fail to pay the fine, you're imprisoned, or legalised gangsters in the form of bailiffs come to clear your house out. Bailiffs have legal authority to enter your home and take away possessions to be sold off. The proceeds of the sale will be used to repay the money owed. No different to how a gangster works.

And, if you evade vehicle excise duty, government officials can come along, take your car away and crush it into a cube! They've even got Stingray mobile-camera units that detect unlicensed vehicles on the move. You face a fine of up to £1,000 for a private car or motorcycle and up to £23,000 for a heavy goods vehicle.

Should you drive over the speed limit and get caught, you also face taxation and the prospect of being chased by legalised gangsters to recover goods from your home to help pay off any unpaid fine. Park in the wrong place and again you're taxed. Motor-insurance premium tax is another sneaky way the government punish you.

We're all trapped by taxation, and legalised thuggery isn't far behind. Stamp duty on property comes into force at a low ceiling, yet property prices go up relentlessly. Who's the thief? The government always get the lion's share of the spoils. They make billions in duty on fuel, fags and booze. New stealth taxes have rocketed like there's no tomorrow!

With all this going on, how can you have faith in the laws of society? You pay your taxes and in return you expect to have clean streets, but often you don't even get that. Calls to the emergency services have hit saturation point, so it can often take the police, in particular, hours to respond. All in all, we are given a pathetic service, considering how much we are taxed; yet we just accept it.

I've had it with that whole tribal thing where you all piss in the same pot and then get a pittance in return for your hard-earned money. People pay me just to have my name hung above the door of their business premises to ward off trouble. I don't see them hanging the name of the local chief constable over the door!

Instant justice is a dish best served cold, which is what I do when there's a drug dealer around. Let's face it, some of the law are as bent as a butcher's hook. They let drug dealers go free, so long as they've been paid off.

But drug dealers have been moved on faster than a speeding bullet, just because of my intervention. Whole communities have thanked me for my services in exterminating what the police couldn't.

I remember a police officer, seeing my T-shirt emblazoned with the words 'The Number One Tax Man', asking me who this 'Number One Tax Man' was. The Chancellor of the Exchequer, I told them.

1 OUR FRIEND ELECTRIC

I WAS BORN on 16 December 1964 in Coatbridge, in Lanarkshire. There was plenty of 'black stuff' all around and the coalmines led to many ironworks being built and the area becoming the most industrialised in Scotland. But, with all that long gone, Coatbridge is now a little gem of a town.

When I was three years old, my parents, Mary and Jimmy, followed my grandma and other family members in leaving that little community. We crossed the border and settled in a little place in the North-East of England, between Billingham and Hartlepool, an area as steeped in industrial history as Coatbridge. Soon we were living in a tiny cottage, where we stayed for about three years.

I am the oldest of five children, and then there is Robert – we call him Bobby – and then my next brother, who is called Skinny because he was always that way, and the next one is my sister, Catherine, and we call her Katy, and then my youngest brother, Jamie.

Within a week of moving into our new home, I was in bed

with pneumonia. Later my mam told me what the doctor had said: 'I don't think he is going to last the night.'

But I was a fighter, because I got through that night, although I was left suffering from asthma. Now and then, I still get a bit of it, but the weight training and other exercise keeps it at bay. I also suffer with hay fever. I am definitely allergic to cats and horses. It is not the hair itself that causes the reaction, it's the old skin cells that are constantly being shed.

I'm all right with some dogs, but others I'm allergic to. Having two of my own doesn't cause me any trouble. Some days I am completely OK and others, if a dog comes near me, I sneeze. Sometimes I can drink milk and I am fine, but another day I can drink it and get a wheezy chest. It's all a mystery. Certain days in winter it's no problem, but in the summer, with the pollen and the tree sap, it makes my nose run.

When I was young, I panicked a lot about my asthma, but when you are older you learn to breathe better. My mother wouldn't put me on an inhaler, even though the doctors prescribed them, as she believed the old wives' tale that if you get on to them you get addicted to them. Several times there were some very anxious moments when I nearly died and was rushed into hospital and put in an oxygen tent. I always battled through and won. In later years, I credit weight training with giving me a lot of my ability to fight against it.

My father was a pathological gambler. He'd be off laying a bet and losing all of his wages, and sometimes we wouldn't see him for days and weeks on end. Things became so bad that we had to go out into the fields and steal the farmer's potatoes just to survive. Mam would put them in the old type of oven that you see in the black-and-white films. At times our stomachs would growl to be fed because we hadn't eaten for days on end as a result of my father being a waster.

When it became too much for my mother, she would go to my grandma's and get some money, come back home and my uncle would come and stay. Uncle Jerry, only five years older than me, was more like an older brother. He stayed with us a lot and looked after us. Sadly, he has since passed away from cancer.

Our cottage was very basic, with no electricity and no flushing toilets. There were only two little bedrooms and seven of us living there. When you needed to go to the toilet, you had to wade through a mountain of rubbish in the garden and dig a hole.

Although we had running water, there was no electricity to heat it. Bath day was an event in itself, as the water had to be heated up on the gas stove. My mam used to wash our clothes in an old tub with a handle on the side that she used to turn to wring out the water. We were brought up on a wing and prayer, as poor as church mice.

The highlight of our week was when we used to go to our grandma's in Redcar at the weekend. I used to stay with her on my own from time to time. Grandma's house would resound with guttural 'Och ayes', as all my uncles had kept their Scottish accent and there was plenty of rolling the Rs. We kids still had the accent when we went to school in Wolviston, which in those days was just a tiny village outside Middlesbrough, with maybe only 50 or 60 houses, though there were a lot of kids at the school.

At my grandma's we would play in the woods and make tree houses. And when my dad wasn't away giving to philanthropic causes such as the local bookmaker, he used to apply his fatherly skills to building wigwams for us.

Racing around on our imaginary horses, slapping our thighs to make them go faster, we would shoot imaginary bullets at make-believe Red Indians from our wooden guns. Our aim was to save their captives from being scalped, but, of course, the Indians would fight back with their tomahawks, bows and

3

arrows and knives and occasionally wound one of us. When the last Indian was killed, the game was over.

If you told kids about that now, they would laugh at you. I tell my son, Jordan, about the way we lived then and it's obvious he'd be lost without electricity. I might say to him, 'You are in trouble now, get to your room.' Well, I wish I'd had his room when I was a child. He has computers, music and all sorts in there, and nowadays it's not a punishment being sent to your room. But not having things didn't bother us in the 1970s because no one else had a lot either. Then again, we had so little that I was sometimes an outcast at school.

When I was about nine or ten we moved to Hartlepool, to 13 Romaine Park. I had visions of playing with the gangs of neighbourhood kids and revelled at the thought of life in a street.

Best of all, we had electricity! We kids hadn't any notion of what it was, so when you turned it on it was, 'Ah, electric!'

We had the television on all the time. When we lived at the cottage, we had a little black-and-white TV powered by a battery that only lasted two hours before the screen died a charcoal colour. My dad would walk to the garage, which was about a mile away, to get the battery recharged. I remember more than once asking where the telly was and Dad said it was broken and in the shop for repair. But he had pawned it and gambled away what he got for it. One time my mam went down to get the telly and they told her, 'Your husband took it out about three weeks ago.'

At our school in Hartlepool, St Helen's, I used to get bullied a lot and because of this I was always staying away. As the new kid there, and with a Scottish accent, I was desperate to be accepted. All my extended family, like my uncles Taff, John and Frank, lived along the coast at Redcar, and I had no cousins to help me sort things out at school with the bullies.

My grandma and granddad had moved to the North-East of England to escape the rough place they lived in. They had seen how the local children were growing up and turning to crime, so they made the decision to take their family away from all that.

This was similar to how a lot of people from Belfast had moved over here to stop their kids being mixed up in that bullshit of Catholics and Protestants hating each other. Those kids had been brought up hearing adults say, 'You don't like them because they are Protestants' or 'You don't like them because they are Catholics.' They are brainwashed, like robots, and from a few years old it is drummed into them.

Here I was, away from the bad influences but still unable to make inroads into a new life. I was the new kid on the block, plus I was always off school, and like that you can't even make friends. I would be at school six weeks, off six weeks, and then I might be off for two months because I was always bad with my chest, and in and out of hospital in oxygen tents.

I would go to the sanctuary of my grandma's and stay for a few weeks, because in those days you could stay off. It would be great fun to be there, a different world.

I used to walk the four miles to school. Actually, I think it was just under four miles because the criterion for having the school bus pick you up was that you had to live at least four miles away; anything under this and you couldn't get a bus. On that long walk I would think about how I was going to avoid getting bullied, because on the way there used to be a gang of lads, maybe five, six, seven, eight of them, who used to bully me. At school, I used to spend all day thinking how I could get home without them setting about me again. I would work out how to get out of it. One way was to slip through a fence and go along the railway line.

Bullying didn't just mean taking a hiding; they'd call you

names too. Telling your parents was a big no-no! You just didn't tell your parents back then.

My mother had five brothers and five sisters and she was the best fighter out of the lot of them. My uncles used to tell me stories of how, when anyone bullied them at school, she would come down and fill the lad in for them. She was a proper tomboy, they said. They also told me that as kids they had decided that one day they would get their own back on her because when it was her job to look after them she used to bray [beat] them.

So, one day, out of the blue, they all attacked her. Uncle Frank was scared to get her, but Taff was beating her up, along with the others. But after the boys set upon her that time, she got them all back, so their plan backfired on them!

Maybe now you can see why I couldn't tell my parents about being bullied. It certainly would have been useless to involve my mother. She wouldn't have given a monkey's, but would have told me to get out and fucking hit them back, because she was such a fighter herself.

Being off school ill so much of the time, I lacked confidence. When you are always poorly or in hospital, how can you expect to have confidence in yourself? Apart from this, I suffered a lot because I was dyslexic. They didn't know about dyslexia in those days, so the teachers just thought you were as thick as two bricks. It wasn't until I was in my twenties that I realised something was amiss and then, when I was told I had dyslexia, the penny dropped.

I wasn't able to read properly until I was 11 or 12, but I can read anything now. I could just about string my words together but the drawback for me was being Scottish: I used to spell words as they sound when Scots say them, with more Rs and Vs than they actually have. Being put in a lower class because of these difficulties only made me even more of a target for bullies.

OUR FRIEND ELECTRIC

When I was about ten I met this lad called Kevin Richardson, who was four or five years older than me and lived just down the road. He is still a friend now. Sometimes Kevin used to stay with because he didn't want to live with his uncle. My mam looked after him as if he was another brother.

Kevin had a brother, Terry, and both of them could fight for fun. In fact, Terry was always getting locked up for fighting. He used to have whippets and dogs and we used to go rabbiting. He would also go after rabbits on horseback but I couldn't, being allergic to horses. Terry was into all that gypsy type of stuff.

Although Kevin used to look after me, the verbal stuff still hurt me. Soon after I moved to the area kids had started mocking me by calling me 'Hong Kong Phoeey', the cartoon character. But I thought I was brilliant and until I was about ten I just pretended to them that I was a karate expert. I said I had been doing karate for about five years and had learned it at a karate school. As a consequence, they were all scared of me. Unwittingly, this constant scheming made me a strategist. For example, every time I went to my granddad's at the weekend I would just tell the other kids that I was going to my karate classes. That way I used to get peace and quiet. This lasted for about six months, until they sussed me out and I got a good hiding, but you always have to think of plans to avoid trouble or get yourself out of it.

We moved to another house in Hartlepool around the time of the Bay City Rollers. I remember because everyone was wearing those daft trousers and scarves. I stayed friends with Kevin and Terry and we used to wander about through a maze of bridges, under one and then another. Eventually we would come out near Hartlepool beach, where there were pipes that pumped out all this steaming effluent. We would sit there playing; our feet would be white with this stuff and it was red-hot, but it didn't seem dirty. There I was, playing with chemical waste. It must be where I got my strength.

From the beach we used to collect sea coal for our fire at home. Rushing down with an old boneshaker of a bike, we would fill bags up with it and put them on the bike and push it home.

The problem with this sort of coal, which came from the nearby sea collieries, was that it wasn't pure. You would be sitting by the fire when, without any warning, a piece of coal would explode and spit showers of shrapnel into your face. To help overcome this we used to wrap it in paper and mix it up with proper coal. Back in those days just about everyone had a coal fire and some kids used to collect sea coal and sell it at 50p a bag.

Our next move was to 224 Westview Road in Hartlepool. The road is still there, but not the house. We used to play football in the street 24/7 and when I was about 14 I got offered the chance to see if I was good enough to play for Hartlepool, either as a goalkeeper or a striker. I was offered two trials but I never went to either of them because I just didn't have enough belief in myself.

I was still a skinny, gangly kid, but it was around that time that I started to develop more confidence and to fight back. There was this lad who wanted a fight with me and he was one of the so-called best fighters in the school. I ended up throwing a volley of punches at him and within seconds he was on the floor in a screaming mess. This new approach, I decided, was better than running away and hiding around corners, frightened of bullies.

Before long, I had beaten every fighter in the school and everyone in the area. I wasn't going to be pushed around any more. I wasn't taking any shit from the bullies. That was it. I was the hardest lad in the school, but I didn't flaunt it.

I remember enjoying all sorts of things on the telly, but, when

I saw James Cagney films, I wanted to be a gangster. That's the life, I thought. It's better than being bullied. Watching characters like that helped me to turn my life around.

2 CHEMICAL BRI

AFTER A FEW years, we moved out to a little village between Hartlepool and Middlesbrough called Graythorpe. It was a community of about 100 houses where RAF personnel who had served in the war used to live. The houses were nice and I know I sound like an old granddad here, but it *was* the sort of place where you could leave your door open. This wasn't because we didn't have anything to steal, not because there weren't any videos and so on in those days; you could leave a bike outside and not worry about it. I had been given a bike by my uncle. He had pinched it and pedalled it all the way from Redcar to Hartlepool, and that was my Christmas present from him.

This is how it was and we never knew any different. I don't consider people who sell £100 tracksuits at Christmas for £15 to poor people that can't afford the shop price as villains. They make a few quid for themselves, but they are also helping low-income people, many of them on the dole, and those who haven't got the opportunity to compete with the higher echelons of society. The kids get a brilliant Christmas out of it and everyone is happy. Their mums and dads might spend £100 in total, but it would have cost many times more if they had bought the same items at the usual retail price. These tracksuits, like perfume and other products sold on the streets and in pubs, are not stolen, though that doesn't mean they're not counterfeits.

But I am not the trading standards officer, so, as long as people aren't selling drugs or anything harmful, why should I bother? After all, these trademarks that are being counterfeited belong to multi-national companies that employ sweatshop workers, virtually slave labour, in the developing world and make billions of pounds in profits. Look at the way football clubs exploit parents by changing their team-strip designs every two years, just to fleece them as often as they can get away with it.

So long as these counterfeiters are not hurting anyone, let them get on with it. Many people are getting hurt by greedy retail chains that can have a top made for £1 and ask £50 for it. They are the real robbers; they are the ones who are hurting people.

I remember having holes in my shoes when we lived in Westview Road. You would still have to go to school, holes or not. If it was raining you would put on a pair of socks, slip a plastic bag over each foot and then another pair of socks, and then you would use a piece of cardboard, cut to shape, as an insole in your shoe. This elaborate fix-it would last half a day and then there would be the same old hole in your shoe and your feet would be wet. In those days, there were boatloads of kids with holes in their shoes.

At school there was this kid called Paul and he had fucking everything! A new tracksuit one week and then the next week he'd have another tracksuit and bright new football boots. The rest of us would be dressed like Steptoe and Son. No football boots, no shorts, nothing. You would have to go into the gym's lucky-dip bin and get what you could. You would come out for a game of football walking like an ape with a pair of football boots of different sizes. One would be a size eight and the other a five!

You may remember Ken Loach's 1969 film *Kes*, the story of a Barnsley boy called Billy Casper. Well, that was just like me at school: no shorts, worn-out shoes and scruffy plimsolls. I remember getting a new pair of plimsolls, and it was a big thing. But now kids want everything.

It's 'Dad, can you get me those trainers?' A hundred and fifty quid for a pair of trainers or £200 for a tracksuit, as if it was nothing. They just don't appreciate things like we did. I sound like a grumpy old man, I know. When I was a kid, I used to say I'm never going to sound like our dad does, but in the end you do, don't you? I thought, I'm not going to sound like my dad does because he moans all the time, but now I understand where he was coming from.

I remember buying a pair of trainers for 99p in Hartlepool. I'd been walking around in trainers that had an elastic band round them and they were flapping because they were knackered. Your mum would give you the money and you would get a new pair of trainers and you would get them home. You would put them on and throw the old ones in the bin. Oh, you can run faster in these, you think to yourself, because they are new and they've got brand-new white laces, and you get so excited over a pair of new trainers that cost less than £1. But that was how it was: brilliant.

Then the school grants would arrive and off to the shops you would go with your mother. 'Oh, another one with a grant,' they would say in the shop, to show you up, but most people had grants then. We would go to what was called Hartlepool's Service Stores, where they stocked all sorts of stuff and, important for us, they accepted grants.

You may think we were right scroungers, but you have to remember this was Hartlepool in the 1970s – not Knightsbridge. About 70–80 per cent of the school kids received free school meals in those days. When I tell you my dad used to work collecting sea coal on the beach and made £500 a week, you will probably think we were scroungers. But when I tell you he used some of this to support his gambling, and when you remember the size of the family, it might make you see what we had to endure.

The old man used an ex-army Bedford lorry and I remember Allen Jackson, who owned the coal yard, saying, 'Your dad is the best worker.' My dad wasn't huge, only about 12 or 13 stone, and he was one of those people that could have two or three hours' sleep and then go out working all day. I went out with him once, when I was 16, and made 50 quid in one night. When I left school, I was on one of those Youth Training Schemes but in that one night we made more money than the YTS paid me for a week. We collected 50 tons of coal that night. My dad would collect 100 tons of coal in one night – he could get eight to ten tons on a wagon – and get £10 a ton for it. He used to work with a lad called Jimmy Walker and they were the best two workers on the beach.

My dad could sniff coal like a pig can sniff a truffle. He knew where it was and it wouldn't be there for very long.

The tide would go out and then when it came in again the coal would settle on the beach in thin layers. You marked out where it was and you would rake it in and make a mound as big as a large garden shed, and not just one mound but several during a shift. Now and then I'd put a bit of sand in, so we'd get a little bit more for it.

You would scrape it all together and then put it on the wagon. It was like that non-stop, like you were scooping ice cream. That was my dad, all day, just scooping it up. He was superfit. All the others, big lads of 15 and 16 stone, were knackered after five minutes and they had to sit and wait, but my dad worked non-stop. 'They are like machines, your dad and Jimmy Walker,' Allen Jackson told me.

My dad would make £500, killing himself all week, and then he would walk into the betting shop and lose it in two or three hours. I have never, ever gambled – he put me right off.

I didn't approve of leaving kids in the house with no food. We didn't even have the potatoes that we used to get out of the farmer's field when we lived in the cottage to keep us going. You just used to have to do without.

In those days, you used to be given a third of a pint of milk at school each day. I was the milk monitor and you would go round with a crate to one class and there would be 20 or whatever in a class and somebody would be off, so you would keep the milk and when you'd finished you would end up with maybe ten spare bottles. You might give some to the staff for the staff room and keep the rest for yourself.

But regular pocket money was unknown. You might get some money now and then when your mum or dad came home with an extra few quid, but it wasn't like the handouts kids get now.

Graythorpe was all right, as everyone knew everyone. There was a little corner shop and we called the shopkeeper Elsie Bump because you could see the big bump on her head. The old girl was about 70 and she used to sell singles [loose cigarettes]. I never used to smoke them. I tried it once and the taste was horrible; smoking is fucking horrible. I never really drank either. When I got older, about 26 or 27, I did drink, with Lee Duffy, but we'll get to that later.

My grandma passed away when I was living at Graythorpe; I was about 14 or 15. The strange thing is, she went to Scotland on holiday to see some family and died of a heart attack there, where she always said she wanted to be buried.

My uncle Frank was a really good footballer when I was a kid, but he was another one for gambling and it was no good for him. When he was 16, the top five teams – Liverpool, Everton,

Man United, Manchester City and West Bromwich Albion – all sent scouts up to the North-East to see him play, so he must have been good.

Eventually he went to Man United, but he should have gone somewhere smaller first and got used to that, like Rooney did, before going on to a bigger team. But sometimes success just goes to a player's head, like it does with pop stars and film stars. That is what happened to Uncle Frank. He was on £200 or £300 a week, which was a lot in those days, especially for a kid of 16. It was too much too soon.

All of my uncles were fighters. Uncle John could fight a bit and he was a footballer. They were all big lads – except for Frank, who was only 10 or 11 stone, though he could fight too. Fighting was bred into all of them.

When we lived at Graythorpe, we couldn't afford much, so I made a bike up. It was a Chopper frame, Chopper back wheel and a Chopper pair of handlebars, with racing front forks and a racing wheel. I didn't know anything about welding, so I took it to a local forge and had the bits welded together. I thought it was great until I grasped the part that had just been welded and burned my hand! I didn't realise the welding was red-hot!

This bike was the bee's knees, this fucking bike I had made myself. We used to ride our bikes and play football; there was nothing else to do. But I remember we once managed to get a tent and camped on the school field for about six weeks in the summer holidays.

When we moved house again it was for our health. The area was surrounded by chemical-industry works and sometimes the washing hung out on the line would become discoloured. It was bad for your health, the environmental-health people told us. They had to knock our houses down.

3 RANDY CRAWFORD BLUES

WE MOVED TO Seaton Lane. The bottom of the road was rough
... well, they had horses. I said, 'I'm not moving to Seaton Lane
because, when everyone asks me where I live, I'm not going to tell
them Seaton Lane. That's the roughest place in Hartlepool.'

As it turned out, our new house, number 200, was at the
very top of Seaton Lane, near Stockton Road. So, when
people asked where we lived, we would say it was on Stockton
Road, as there was such a stigma attached to the other end of
Seaton Lane.

I wasn't keen at first, but I soon found it was great, because
the girl next door was 15 and so was I. On the other side was
a girl of 16 and then there was 17-year-old Tracy Laughton
and another one of about 14 ½, so there were plenty of girls in
the street.

The first night I was there, I was out in the street talking to the
girls and this lad goes by. He was wearing a Crombie coat and,
as he walked by, he threw a stick in my face.

This dirty lass said, 'You know, I don't think you should mess with him because he is the best fighter. He's called John Redman and he is the best fighter in the area.'

I didn't see this John Redman, who was perhaps a couple of years older than me, for about six months. I was 16 now and I'd started seeing this girl called Sandra Grills who lived down the street. She was my first proper girlfriend and we went out for about four years. I'd got a mouth organ for Christmas and started to learn how to play it, though I never really got far with it. I was on my way to see Sandra, with the mouth organ in my hand, when I spotted Redman. I walked on the other side, just to avoid trouble, as I could see he was either drugged or pissed. He was all over the road and he thought the mouth organ was a knife.

I tried to defuse him, saying, 'It's not a knife, mate, it's a mouth organ.'

'Come on, I'll fight you,' he goaded me.

I headbutted him and he crashed to the floor. Reaching down and seizing him by the ear, I pulled him up and thrust my knee into his face and he went down like a broken lift. I held his head down with my well-placed boot on his head. He was squealing like a pig.

My mum came and quipped, 'What's that on the floor?'

I replied, 'Well, he is causing trouble.'

By this time, she knew I wasn't taking any shit any more and I was beating the best fighters. I mean, he was about 17 ½ or 18 then and I was about 16. In that age group, he was the best fighter and I brayed him. But then he told everyone that I had pulled a knife on him – dickhead.

This girl, Denise Wakeland, said to me, 'You were having him, but I'm not going to talk to people with knives.'

'It was a mouth organ!' I said.

I showed her it because I still had it in my pocket and she started talking to me again.

When I left school, I went for a job interview and in those days it was those YTS, where you only got £23.50 a week – slave labour. This was another government con. You went on to a YTS for six months and this didn't count as working, but when it came to tallying up the unemployment figures you were classed as working and not one of the millions of unemployed. Fiddling the figures? They are the biggest gangsters walking.

Anyway, under the YTS I got a job in a forge. The foreman was a bit of a bully because three other lads that had been there had been filled in, but I wasn't fucking bothered. He was about 25 years old, not massive, about 13 stone, while I was about 11 stone. Obviously, he was a man and I was only a kid of 16.

The boss, Peter, was all right, and it wasn't hard work, mainly sweeping up and making the coffee and putting things away, drilling things and bullshit like that. But we still had to get up and go to fucking work every day. It was three miles and you would get the standard YTS rate of £23.50 a week for working eight or nine hours a day. It took half an hour to get there and half an hour to get back, so you are talking about ten hours a day for fucking 50 pence an hour or something.

So one day I'm working and young Tilly says, 'Blokes, you can get away now, you can get away, fella.'

You would have these pieces of metal that you would put on a runner and they would be pushed out and formed into something like a letterbox. We were packaging these up and this bloke came up and spat, 'Here, don't be shutting, I'm the boss.'

I replied frostily, 'Peter said we can shut up and he's the owner ...'

'I'll fucking give you a bat in the mouth in a minute, you cheeky little cunt,' he threatened.

'Well, I would like to fucking see you try,' I told him.

There was this barrel where you would put offcuts of metal. While he was telling me to come and get him, I picked a metal bar up from the barrel and fucking brayed the cunt all over with it.

I broke his arm and four of his ribs. In a feeble attempt at pulling some of the glory back, he tried punching me in the face. I am not a bully but I'm not going to get bullied by any fucker.

Obviously, I got the sack. After being unemployed for a short spell, I got a job with British Steel, same type of thing, working on a training course for ten weeks. My wages had now gone up to £25 a week! I wasn't going to be able to afford a boat on the Costa del Sol on this dramatic increase in income. It was even fucking further to walk every day, so I thought, Well, I'm going to get a motorbike. I started saving up for this one, which was about £50.

Then my dad said, 'I'll give you £1 an hour if you come on the beach.' He was on £10 an hour and he was going to give me £1 an hour out of his wages to help him and Jimmy Walker and another lad. We got 50 tons of coal in one night, about 12, 14 hours' work. After a night like that, my dad would come home and say, 'Are you ready again?' I couldn't get up, I was totally fucking gone, I couldn't do any more work. But soon I had made more than the money I needed for the bike.

I had earned £120 and I saw this bike in the paper for £125, so I went down with my dad and we got it for 120 quid. It was a 125-cc and I was flying about. Motorbikes back then weren't governed for speed, and it could do 90 mph!

We were all getting on with my dad now because he wasn't gambling, or only now and then. My mam had paranoia and odd thoughts in her head, and she would sometimes go on mad drinking sprees and you wouldn't see her for two or three days. She used to go to Redcar on Thursday, Friday, Saturday and come home on Sunday. She would be in bed recovering for two days and then be back on it again. Now it was my dad's turn to suffer. He had to make our porridge in the morning and get the others off to school.

You could give him a hammer, some nails and a lump of wood and he could build you a house; he can do anything. My brother Jamie – he's a carpenter – he's the same. Ask him to make anything out of wood or steel and he can do it; he is brilliant with his hands.

My dad would do daft things, like his gambling and drinking, and you would get up in the morning and Mam and him would be arguing. Then when you came home there would be this Randy Crawford record playing, and one night she played it about 25 times and I felt like smashing it.

My brother Bobby would say, 'For fuck's sake, she's not going to play that fucking record again!'

We used to put toilet paper in our ears so we could fall asleep. I would like to kick Randy Crawford right in the fucking fanny. I think, if they kept playing that record in the police station like they did at home, I'd say, 'I'll tell you everything, just don't play it again, please.'

4 FIXING ON WINNING

I WAS GETTING about on my motorbike and still going out with Sandra. We would go out on the bike for a few hours and then head home. Money was nothing to us then, we were just happy.

The council were modernising the houses, so we had to move into another street for a while. Then Sandra and I decided, when we were 17, 18, to get a house together in Billingham.

We were living together and we got an Alsatian; we named her Sadie. I have always loved dogs and looked after them. You see these scumbags hurting animals, cats sometimes. I don't like cats, but I wouldn't hurt animals. You see these people who shoot horses in the field with their air rifles. They are the vermin, they want really braying. Villains who shoot each other, they are different; they are doing that because they might get killed otherwise. If someone is planning to shoot you, well, you take them out before they take you out.

But someone looking after an animal and then hurting it like they were just lighting a fags turns my stomach; so does hurting old people. I have knocked out quite a few of these scumbags who harm animals. I don't even kill spiders, I put them all out. I wouldn't kill anything like that. Life is precious. The way I look at religion is, if there is something good, I would rather be on the good side than on the devil's.

I wouldn't say it's the winning side because you get these fucking idiots that are evil bastards praying to the devil. Now I didn't go to church or Sunday school, even though my family are Catholics. But what I am saying is I don't think you have to go to church to be a good person.

Unlike some people, I don't carry a cross of righteousness stoically and steadfastly. Some lads went into this religious place the other day and one had been really bad on coke and heroin, but they got him off both. I say it is a good thing. If you pray to something that is not there but it gets you off drugs anyway or it stops you being suicidal, to me it has got to be a good thing.

Even if God doesn't exist, it still helps some people who have mental breakdowns, because they go there and it makes them better. I'm not saying anything is true or untrue, I'm sceptical, but I wouldn't knock it. I would say, good on them if it is making them happy in their life and making their family happier. It's better than gambling or taking drugs all weekend and not providing for your kids.

What really annoys me, the more I think about religion, is these fucking do-gooders who are all goody-goody but are braying or interfering with their own kids at home. Or these warped old nuns and monks sexually abusing kids they are responsible for. You must get the devil out of you and all that! They are just evil bastards.

There was a film, based on a true story, where these kids in an Irish school have been stealing and playing hookey and the priest is raping a young boy. In another one, about nuns, Pierce Brosnan played the father of two little girls who were taken from him because he couldn't provide for them, as he was a drunk. But then he got himself on his feet and looked after them, but he found the nuns had been bastards to the kids, beating them with fucking sticks and rulers. To me, priests and nuns like that are cowards.

The way we lived as kids wouldn't be acceptable these days. Can you imagine it? Our father was a gambler, seven of us living in a two-bedroomed cottage with no electricity. Nowadays your kids would be taken off you and put into care. There would be a demand for justice and vigilance by some do-gooder.

I remember, if we got into trouble, Mum would bray us – and I mean fucking brayed. If you did that today, you could go to jail. I am not saying it is a good thing, because I would never hit Jordan. If he ever misbehaves, I say I'm going to fucking bray you in a minute and he gets threatened every day, but he never gets touched. He isn't a bad kid, he doesn't get into trouble.

I remember breaking into a factory when we were kids and it was more like playing or messing about, but I haven't got a record for stealing or for burglary. We didn't get much, so we would pinch from the shops, but we never got caught for anything like that. It was fucking bad, though, having soaking wet feet. Now it's funny but at the time it wasn't. There will still be kids out there with holes in their shoes, but not many and there's no excuse. Food has never been so cheap. Everything is so cheap. We must be living in a better time: everybody has got a car or a phone, though every phone I get the police keep bugging it.

Sandra and I lived in Billingham for about six months, but we didn't know anybody there. I remember a trip to the seaside and we thought we were going into this place to see a film. Inside, everyone is sitting there with dicky bows and white shirts and I'm sitting there with a pair of cowboy boots, denim jeans and denim jacket on and Sandra is sitting there not looking smart either. We thought we were only going to the pictures but it was a play with Lorraine Chase in it. We'd got in the wrong queue, but it was good. My first and probably last foray into the theatre.

It was not long before Sandra and I split up, and soon afterwards I started weight training. I was about 18 or 19 and living back at Seaton Lane. I wanted to get into weights because I had seen *The Incredible Hulk* and things like that on the telly. It sounds corny now, but I wanted to be massive. When I saw the film *Pumping Iron* for the first time, I thought, Fucking hell, I would love to be like that. Look at the size of him!

My uncle Tam was a gambler, a bad gambler, like my dad. He would be up five grand and then lose the fucking lot. I remember him going to London, making £10,000. He went down there for about three months and within three weeks of coming home he had blown it all. He would go in the betting shop every day, putting every penny on the horses.

He had borrowed so much money off my mum, 100 or 150 quid, and he couldn't pay, so he said, 'Look, Mary, I've got a set of weights ... take them for the money.'

I remembered the weights because I had been to his girlfriend's with him in Redcar and I did a little bit of training on the weights he had there. My uncle had an old bench with a little bit of carpet on, two dumb-bells and about 150 or 160 pounds in weights.

I trained diligently every day for about an hour and a half or two hours, but I didn't realise I was doing too much. My appetite went through the roof, so I ate a lot, but I still overtrained and I was still playing football too. Naturally, I didn't put any weight on.

After I'd been training for about a year or two, I was this rock-hard Bruce Lee type, solid abs and all that. I turned the spare bedroom into a gym, just with the bench and a few weights and got another set of dumb-bells and I would just be bench-pressing all the time. But I never had a big body; I was thin and still only 12 stone.

I also training on the weights at my uncle Tam's place and I went to Chapel Gym, which had been converted from a church. This had a real blood-and-guts atmosphere, what with the old imperial weights as opposed to the metric weights they use now. It was like the old *Rocky* film. I saw these lads, Peter Rayne and Terry Cooper, who had both been in body-building competitions. To me, they were Schwarzenegger doubles: Terry was just over 16 ½ stone and Peter was 14 ½ or 15 stone. To me, they were as huge as a small aircraft hangar. They bristled with rippling muscle. Their arms were 18 inches in girth and they had 50-inch chests. Massive!

I wanted to be like them. I was training like there was no tomorrow. I felt empowered by the discipline of the weights. I was there every day, six days a week. In those days, I used to train chest, back and biceps on a Monday, then shoulders, triceps and calves on a Tuesday and then rotate. It was too much, but I didn't realise. Now I only train them once a week.

In Redcar, where my uncle lived, this lad called Chip, a drunkard, was offering a rundown council flat in a low-demand area known as the Courts, in the Lakes Estate. In fact, the place wasn't too bad then, so I took the flat. It was only little but it had everything. Most important of all was the electric meter. You'd put a pin in it to stop it clocking up.

And you would be claiming on the dole. At that time, you could claim £10 a night for bed and breakfast because there was a law saying you could have bed and breakfast in a seaside town. What happened is that Margaret Thatcher stopped it, saying that you could only have six weeks in each town. So, with me having asthma, I got a letter from the doctor saying that I couldn't be moving around to different places or damp places. I played on it a bit.

Anyway, some lad took Thatcher to court over it and he won his case, so I got some back money, about two grand, and spent it all on training and eating better food. Because I couldn't drive, I got myself a racing bike. I got myself a job parking cars at Redcar racecourse. For that, I used to get about seven quid a day. I got another job there as well: every time there was a photo finish I took the shot, and I got seven quid for that too.

When I finished my shift at the course, I would steadfastly go to the gym. By now, I was putting a bit of weight on. The training was starting to pay dividends and I was up to around 14 ½ stone at the age of 19. I even managed to get myself a job at the gym as a training instructor. I met these people from a farm and I used to get about 150 eggs a week off them. I used to eat 30 a day! I would have ten scrambled eggs for breakfast and slices of toast with porridge. I could eat three times as much then as I can now, but when you are younger you eat more.

A girl I knew was a hairdresser, so she used to cut my hair, and I was starting to get to know other people. I was getting bigger and bigger and bigger while at Anthony Berg's gym. Then I started training at another gym, the Olympia, an elite place and probably the best gym in Teesside now, something like a Gold's gym. The owner was Don Williams and what a fucking moaner he was! You weren't allowed to bang the weights. In the old days, you used to throw the weights back.

Although I was aware what steroids were, I had never taken anything like that, so I stayed off them and I trained at a gym with a lad called Tony Buxton, who was the training instructor there. He was about 15 ½ stone, he was ripped and shredded and he looked really good. Tony helped me along and I trained with him for a few years.

After that, I trained with a lad called George Fawcett, who

has just won Over-50s Mister Britain. We would train twice a day. When we went out on the town together they used to say, 'Oh, look, Twit and Twat,' because we were from the local Gold's gym.

I promised myself that I would work up to show standards. There was only ten days before a body-building competition I was keen to enter. You can diet in ten days and lose a stone. I went in for this contest and weighed in at 14 stone and four pounds; I had dropped over a stone, as planned. It was the Mr England at Gateshead, run by Matty Boroughs, himself a former champion body-builder. When I got there, the stadium was packed.

I had entered the Under-21s competition and 21 guys were vying for the title. Back in those days, it was a massive contest because everyone wanted to be a body-builder.

I can tell you, it took some guts and heart to stand up on stage with just a pair of fucking underpants on, greased up, in front of 2,000 people, with cameras on you.

I didn't win but I came fifth or sixth.

I went on to enter the Mr Skegness competition, where I was fourth or fifth. Next came the Mr Crowtree competition at the local leisure centre, with about 20 in the line-up. All my uncles were there to see me, so I had to do well. But there I realised that it was all about who you knew!

The lad who was on stage with me, I thought I was better than him, and everyone else knew I was. I'm not blowing my own trumpet but, although the lad who won was excellent, I was sure I was in the first two or three and I was placed a disheartening fifth.

The lad who came second, his dad was one of the judges. I knew then that you couldn't win with odds like that stacked against you. So I thought, Fuck this body-building malarkey.

I didn't expect to win, but I thought I was doing better than him and when I was ranked fifth there were about 200 people booing at the result. But at least I'd been up there and had a taste of it.

I went on training hard and the most I ever weighed was 23 stone and 10 pounds, which was getting ridiculous. The only good thing I can say about being obsessive was that you were never happy, you were still hungry to achieve more.

Next year I will have been training for 25 years and I'm still going strong. But you would be down in weight one month, to 23 stone, and then you would go on the gear (steroids) and then come off and you might go back down to 21, which is what I am now.

The drawback is, when you get an illness, you still want to do it and to stay hungry. You get fighters wanting to be the best and I can understand why Mike Tyson just wouldn't yield his title. It is hard to train, it is hard when you are getting there and it's even harder to stay there.

5 THE EAGLE DOES NOT CHASE AFTER FLIES

SOON AFTER LOSING these competitions, I took a doorman's job and changed my training regime. Things have to be right when you train or what's the use of training? It is like when I went to jail: I was 22 ½ stone and when I came out I was a skeletal 18 stone! There were a few people having a go at me in prison, but I was still the top fucking fighter and I was still strong. It was just you weren't taking in as much food and you were eating shit food. I was still training hard, doing an hour's circuit a night. I was running about like a lunatic, doing circuits and 500 sit-ups a day and 500 press-ups and mad things like that, but when you're in jail there is nothing else to do.

Back to my life outside: I was now in training with George Fawcett and I was doing a few competitions. John Garland was another lad who trained with us.

I was about 20 when I first worked on the doors, at a place in Redcar called Leo's that stayed open until 1am. I asked for the job and the lad who gave me it was called Peter Rhymes. I worked with Jeff Robinson, who was sound as a pound and about ten years older than me.

I was green as grass in this job. I'd never gone to nightclubs in my teens; I never drank, never took drugs. I was just a lad who had trained all my life and there I was on the nightclub scene working the door. I remember clearly the first fight I had to break up. You are nervous because you don't know what to do – not scared, just nervous. There was this big lad, about 15 stone, who grabbed me and was pulling me. I went to throw him out but he grabbed a rail and I couldn't get him down. I didn't know what to do because I didn't know how to throw punches properly as they didn't train you in boxing and I just did weights.

Grabbing at him wildly, I put him out but he ran at me, so I nutted him and he fell to the floor like a stuffed doll and that was it. After that, there was fight after fight after fight to deal with, but I was still wrestling because I didn't know how to punch. I was just a brute of a lump!

I stayed at Leo's for several years and I was doing three jobs, still working at the racecourse and at the gym as well. I was pulling in about £200 a week – a lot of money 20 years ago. Every penny went on training and eating. I only paid a tenner a week for my flat, remember, because it was a lad's council flat.

About £150 a week went on food. I was constantly eating and getting bigger. I used to go and buy the stupidest things, like protein and all sorts of vitamins. I used to take about 40, 50 vitamin tablets a day. It was all bullshit, because with all the food you are eating you don't need all those tablets: you are getting enough from the food. Your body can only handle about 20 grams of protein in one meal, so what's the point of having 100 grams when you can only digest 20?

It is only in the last ten years that I've got into proper dieting. When you eat every two or three hours you don't need to eat massive dinners with 20 eggs and so on. People think that you have to eat big meals, but you are better off with six normal meals than three big meals.

When I first started training, I was doing sets of 'tens'. We didn't know about all these things like triple drops and mid-training, but we were still strong. I was a rock-solid 14 stone at 20, which is a lot of weight.

I trained in the Olympia and at the time I remember Dave Williams was the best fighter in the area, and, I would say, he was like a body-builder called Tim Belknap, an old-school body-builder. Williams was 15, 16 stone and about five foot eight, with massive forearms, and he had punched George, my mate. He was the best fighter in the area and he beat Pete Hoe, who was the best fighter in Eston [in Middlesbrough]; he beat him twice and was the kiddie in the area.

I remember, when I was 19 or 20, spilling Williams's drink at the nightclub and he tried to bully me. He brayed everyone, and he could fight. He had done a bit of boxing and he was the best fighter locally for years.

My mate, John Garland, was Scottish, and I worked with him on the door at Leo's for years. But then I nutted someone and dropped him and fractured his skull and the police were after me. So I moved to Philmores, working on the door Monday, Thursday, Friday and Saturday. Everyone got on with me, but the first person to say something wrong, I would knock them out.

I think it was partly a lack of confidence, because when you're older you get cockier, and you think, Well, I could destroy you if I wanted to but I don't have to. You were paranoid and you wanted to defeat them to show them that you were the best. Just like Tyson wanted to be the best fighter in the world when he was 20. But when you get older you are not as bothered. People bump into you now and you are not as bothered, but then it was, 'Who are you fucking pushing?'

I moved on to the Top Deck and various other clubs; nearly every club in Redcar in fact. Then I started working in a pub and seeing this girl and when I fell out with her I stayed at my mate Little Frankie Atherton's house. A lovely bloke, he is about 70 now. Frankie taught me loads, how to box, how to throw punches, because he was a professional fighter when he was younger. He was only 17 when he became a boxer. He was married but his wife fucked off and he had kids to look after, and he came to live in Redcar.

When I was about 23, I went to Ray Hood's gym in Lingdale and started boxing there. I wanted to be a boxer but I just couldn't get my weight down enough. I managed to get down to about 17 stone, though that was still a lot for a heavyweight to carry back then.

I lost a fight I had at 24 because the lad was one of those people who would jump and move all the time. I would have knocked him out if he'd stood still. I lost the fucking fight on points and I thought, This is not for me. I was better just grabbing hold of them and fucking braying them. I wanted to bash the bastards and smash their faces off the floor and pull their fucking arms out or bite their noses off. If it had been a street fight where you're standing fighting, I would have won the fight because you couldn't have got away, but the referee used to pull you all the time. It was just fucking shit. So I went back to about 19 stone and I was working in Philmores for a while. It's now a hotel and bar.

Philmores was a funny old nightclub where you would be fucking fighting with everyone. It was along the coast from Redcar, in Saltburn, an agricultural area with a lot of farmers wanting to fight. I was assigned the upstairs part, working on my own. There were six men on the door, so I was fighting the whole fucking nightclub on my own. I would be fighting every fucker and knocking them all out. By now, I was getting a big reputation. I beat everybody in Redcar and now I beat everybody in Saltburn too.

People used to say, 'You're not that fucking hard.'

I remember this lad came up to me and said, 'You're a big lad, but I bet you can't move fast ...'

Boom! My fist travelled from 0 to 60 mph in a millisecond and I fucking knocked him out with my right hand.

When he woke up I asked, 'Was that fast enough for you?'

Nowadays that wouldn't bother me, but back then it was, 'Look, you daft cunt, who are you talking to?' and I just hit him. You are more aggressive when you are younger, more like a warrior, but when you get older you realise how much you have got to lose. Without controlling my punches, a man of my size could kill with one blow! When you are young, you are not worried about it.

I have knocked down a lot of people, fractured their skulls, broken their jaws and put them in comas. I have put legs and arms out and bitten off people's noses, lips and ears. When you are doing that, the last thing you are thinking about is the judge sending you to prison. The way I looked at it was, even if I got jail for it, that was better than being beaten. No, that wouldn't matter: you just think, Fuck that, he is going to try to do it to me.

There has to be a point, though, where you change from being careless to being careful. You don't know how good you are because you think, Well, I might have been lucky there, but you can't be lucky in the middle of your fucking fight. There is a big difference between thinking, or hoping, you're good and actually *knowing* how good you are. It's being able to assess this that makes all the difference.

Nowadays, I know I can beat anybody and that is what is firmly in my mind, but in those days I didn't carry such a positive thought with me. When you are young and somebody says something that gets to you, you think you have to prove something. You go round punching people for just that reason.

I never ever lost a fight. No matter who it was that I came up against, I beat them. Sometimes it would be easy, sometimes it would be hard and sometimes I would come out with a black eye and have a broken cheekbone or broken nose. I have never had a broken jaw, never been knocked out. I always used to win, no matter whether the fight was sloppy or I knocked them out with one shot. I might have a fight with someone weighing 20 stone. Boom! They would be knocked out. Or I might fight someone of 14 stone and it would take about a dozen punches because you can't always get your best shot in easily. Later on, you learn all this and so you don't lose, you go in and use all your adrenalin and the fight is over within a minute.

Now I don't think there is anybody in the country that could beat me, and people would say things like, 'Nobody in Teesside could beat you.' They would say that I would be one of the top-ten unlicensed fighters in Britain. This was no-holds-barred, anything-goes fighting. Nobody would beat me, they said, because I was just so fast with my hands and had been hit by the best fighters. You have taught the best fighters and you have beaten the best fighters, they would say. You have been hit with bars and they still couldn't knock you out. It's not just luck, is it? It can't be fucking luck all the time: hundreds and hundreds of fights and I have beaten them all.

So, I'm working in Philmores, I'm about 24 and I'm still boxing and doing the weights. I wouldn't say I was a great boxer, because I wasn't, but my hand speed was phenomenal for my size.

I remember Lee Duffy saying to me, 'How do you have hand speed that fast and be that big? You beat the laws of physics!'

I went to Little Frankie's house. How he could work up in Spennymoor, I don't know. It was a fucking nightmare! Dead rough. For those who don't know it, Spennymoor is just a little village, but it is a village with a lot of boxers all trained for fighting and a lot of gypsies from Bishop Auckland and places like that – a whole load of good fighters. Also, when I was a kid a lot of National Front people lived there.

I met this man called John Black, the best fighter in Middlesbrough, and got a job with him. We worked from his house with John Watson, Paul Cook and Gerry Russell. There were about 20 doorman in all but only seven worked on the door at one time, and they called us 'The Magnificent Seven'.

On my first night we were standing at the door and these wankers at the front of the queue were throwing stones and coins at us and I said, 'Fuck this!'

I jumped out and brayed six lads, one after the other, and knocked them on their arses.

One lad shouted at me, 'You knocked me down, but you didn't hurt me,' and as he was running across the road a fucking car knocked him over and broke both his legs.

Later, a copper came by on his beat and told me the ironic thing was that it was the lad's own car. It was his mate who was coming to pick him up and he knocked him over and broke his fucking legs. No, I thought, I didn't hurt you, but that fucking hurt, didn't it?

For fighting, that club, the Top Hat, was probably the roughest I ever worked in. I had never seen anything like it. It was a pub downstairs and you would go upstairs and it was full of gypsies; 20 would come to the door and they were fucking game. Then one night about 20 fucking bikers turned up and we fought with the lot of them.

I had drink thrown in my eyes – a pro bar-fighter's ploy. I think it was just cider or something but I could hardly fucking see and I was getting hit with all sorts. I was trying to open my eyes to fight. Anyway, we were dropping people left, right and centre. Chairs were bouncing off my head, Grolsch bottles and fucking glasses, and girls were throwing things at you. We were punching away like in the cowboy films and it was just mad.

I also worked at another nightclub for John, the Down Town in Stockton, when he owned that. That was where I met Amanda, my wife. I used to work in Down Town first and then I would go to Water Front to make sure everything was all right there, and then to Henry Africa's, which was a big nightclub and a rough place because it was in a tough area of Stockton. Then we would go on to Spennymoor and later, on the way back, I would pop into the nightclubs in Billingham. I used to do five or six clubs in total, making sure they were all right.

One time when we were working in Henry Africa's there were maybe 10 or 12 army lads in there. They were standing there and this band was on, a bit like Hot Chocolate, and this woman said, 'I want to go backstage and see them.'

My eyes caught hers and I told her, 'Well, you can't, they've come straight here from another gig and they just want to get away.'

She insisted, 'I want to go in. I'm coming in. I've paid.'

As she tried to hit me with a glass, I pushed her and she went down. Then her boyfriend came over and I knocked him out and dragged him and his girlfriend out of the place. Just as the eagle does not chase after flies, I left them lying there.

It was raining cats and dogs and the pair of them were strewn like discarded party poppers in the puddle outside. When I walked back in, this army lad ranted, 'I'd like to see you do that to the paratroopers!'

'Fuck off, you knobhead,' I shouted at him.

He ran at me and … boom! I hit him and he went down like a broken statue. Next, I gave his mate a bare-knuckle ride and

6 WRECKING CREW

THE WAY THE media portrays a goodie is quite complex. The goodies are usually the fucking baddies! In the police nowadays, there is more corruption than there has ever been and, even in little places like this, it's unbelievable. In a way, you can't blame them. Some get in the region of £400 a week and when a drug dealer says, 'I'll give you a grand a week if you help me out and don't get me nicked,' they succumb. They are going to do it or they are going to take, say, a few kilos of coke in a raid and keep some to sell on. It's happening all over. It's the times we are living in.

Once we went to Leeds to work with John because the number-one man down there, Marco, had all the doors under his control; his doorman had brayed this mob with sticks or something at this club called the Warehouse.

I worked there for a few weekends and there were only about four of us on the door, so we were taking a chance. We must have had some bottle to go and work on a fucking door in Leeds, where they were all big bastards running about and we had to search them for guns and knives, looking in their bags on their way in. It was that type of club. We worked there for a few weekends, but there was no real trouble and, whatever there was, we dealt with it.

We weren't bothered: we would go any place, any time and work anywhere, so we became known as the Martini Bunch, after the ad of the time. In contrast, there were doormen like Viv Graham, who lived in Newcastle, who would stay in his own clique and you would never see him go to Sunderland or Middlesbrough to work. Then you would get people like Lee Duffy, who would work anywhere and didn't give a fuck. He would go to Manchester, and he had no fear of anyone or anything. Maybe they should have called him the Martini Man!

For people like Viv Graham, I think it was the fear of losing that meant more to him than anything else.

I have no such fear of losing. I once got beaten and it is good to lose in a way, as then you know what's around, because I had never lost a fight before. I had been on ecstasy and drinking alcohol for two fucking hell-raising days, and when I went outside with a lad he beat me straight away.

I beat myself. If I had never taken those drugs and had trained for six months, I could still have gone out and fought. You can't do it; you have got to train all the time.

I was working on the door in Henry Africa's and places like that. We weren't frightened to work anywhere, because we had done the door in Spennymoor and Leeds.

I remember in Billingham there was this ginger lad who ran most of the town with another kid and he came looking for an argument, so I gave him my WMD, a steaming left hook, in the toilet and knocked him out. And he was supposed to be one of the best fighters in Billingham!

In Spennymoor, three doormen who worked for Tuxedos – I think it was – came into the club. The first one of the group was about 15 stone, and they all wore these waiter-type jackets, like those little male stripper's jackets.

One of them gave it the large and muttered, 'Tux.'

'What is Tux, mate?' I enquired.

'We are doormen and we are coming in,' he bragged.

'Here, have some fucking respect, mate,' I told him. 'If you had asked properly instead of using a turd for a head, then you would have got in. You are fucking paying now, Don fucking Corleone.'

I'd give them Tux all right: tucks up in a hospital bed! The adrenalin kicked in at 20,000 rpm. It's no good pretending you're a fighter and giving it the large. That's like wearing a condom with a limp dick!

They were blissfully unaware of what was about to happen to them. Turned on by the prospect of smashing them into oblivion, I put on a spectacular display of violence. I gave the first guy a chopping right hand to the face that was catastrophic for him and then I inflicted pain on the other two with a fast cluster of bare-knuckle rides, and knocked both of them out. The place looked like a scene from one of those staged road accidents.

As they were lying on the floor, half-unconscious, trying to get to their feet, I growled, 'You want to fucking grow up. Fucking get them out.'

That was the end of those fucking Tux. I wouldn't have any shit, and I remember working on the door there and I had beaten everyone. I remember this doorman came in – I can't recall his first name – and bragged, 'I'm so-and-so Ellis. I've had 67 fights and have only lost two.'

I'll give him credit: he was a game fucker and as near to Conan the Barbarian as you can get. I gave him a slice of the Tax Man with a blasting right hook and told him, 'Well, that's three you've lost now.'

And then his brother jumped in and I banged him too, and both of them were lying knocked out in the passageway. They were the best fighters in Spennymoor and had turned pro, I think. They would awake feeling a little sore!

Another one, called Green, was a light heavyweight and when I went to fight him he ran off. You have got to remember: in the boxing ring you can call out and have the towel thrown in, you are only getting punched with spongy gloves and you have got a referee pulling you apart. Oh, and you've got the bell to sound the one-minute rest period at the end of each round.

That's all well and good in the ring, but in the urban jungle there is none of that. There are people with knives and you have just got to use your instincts. All that boxing stuff goes out of the window when someone weighing 20 stone or more grabs hold of you or you're up against someone who is very strong.

Some boxers are very fast but, when they are in close-quarters fighting and are grabbed hold of, they can't fight; they think, What am I going to do now? They are only trained to run about, skip and jump. Outside the ring, you can bang them like a shithouse door in the wind and then sidestep the other way and they can't move their feet or their hands. You can do that as well as they can, maybe not quite as well, but if you've done boxing it's an advantage.

You need to do a little bit of everything to be the best all-rounder. I remember Bob Cumber. I still know him because he was another one I could beat. Bob was a karate expert six or seven times and weighed in at 13 stone. He said to me, 'No matter how much karate I know, you can grab me and I'm fucked because you'll just pick me up and throw me about like a rag doll. I can't throw you over me, I can't fucking grab your wrist and pull you around, I can't slide you, I can't sweep you because you are too big. It's impossible. All that karate goes out of the window.'

WRECKING CREW

I once knocked out a world champion kick-boxer outside Henry Africa's. He was jumping about and I hit him with my piledriver of a left hook and knocked him fucking clean out. There he was, knocked out on the floor alongside the trophy that he had just won that night. His trophy looked nice, though.

It all started when he was just standing there like a damp squib and I said, 'You can't come in wearing trainers.'

There was a load of them and they had big heads because he had just won the fight, and he came up the steps trying to be clever, saying, 'Well, I have got a trophy and they like the trophy and I just want to ...'

My body language was screaming at him to shut up and I just went bumph! Fuck off! before he could even get hold of me. He never had a chance to tell me the rest of the story. I just knocked him out, and then threw his trainers on to the roof.

That was a favourite trick, taking people's shoes and socks and throwing them over the telephone lines. Maybe they could feel how I felt when I was a kid with no shoes or socks.

On the door at Spennymoor, I had beaten loads of people by the time I'd been there about three months. I destroyed everyone, knocking them out with one punch. In an effort to dethrone me, some of them brought this gypsy into the equation. In those days, you could get a pie and pea licence; I don't know if they do them now. You could stay open until twelve o'clock on a Sunday, but you had to stop serving at half-past ten, I think. Talk about binge drinking, this was binge buying! People would buy three or four pints and sit down with them and keep a pint and be out until midnight and you would have to serve the pie and peas, though that cost fucking pennies. The club would make good money, so we used to work on the door on a Sunday. Only two of us used to get paid for it, but we would all come down because we were that loyal to each other, so there were six or seven of us on the door, five doing it for nothing. John's doormen would come for a night out and we would all go down there and mess about.

Although this was a club you had to sign in, it may as well just have been a weigh-in to get passed to come in... that's how rough it was.

I was working alongside Little Frankie Atherton when this six-foot-eleven bloke came to the door. I am six-three and he was bigger than the doorframe. He had a big beard and big gold sovereigns on his fingers. But, although he was big, he wasn't a muscular type of guy – more like a basketball player. He weighed about 20 stone. Back then, I wasn't massive, maybe 18 stone, but because I was boxing I was fast and very, very strong.

I put my hand on the door and with my chin resting on my shoulder I said, 'You can't get in, mate. Last orders have been called.'

He stood eyeballing me and he seethed, 'Well, I'm coming in.'

Then he grabbed me, but John intervened and told me, 'Let him in.'

'Last orders have gone!' I said.

But in he came anyway. He had to duck his gargantuan frame down so he could get in, and he grunted in a big, deep voice. Inside, in the passageway, there was a cornice near the top of the wall and his head was higher than that.

He stood there, turned around and said, 'You are a cheeky cunt, you, like.'

I had a nice surprise in store for him, as up until then my day had been panning out fine. For what was about to happen, you would need a widescreen TV to view it in all its glory. I sprang at him, taking the steam out of him as I grabbed him in a vicelike grip with my left hand. I threw a hugely dangerous right uppercut that lifted him clean off his size-13 feet, and he nearly went through the ceiling. This colossus of a man fell back and slid down the wall like peeling wallpaper. That put paid to Lurch.

I recall another bizarre incident. We used to have a book by the door and you would sign your name, say, 'Steve Richards, Gateshead', so people would sign in as 'John Smith, S Moor', which was short for Spennymoor.

This man signed his name as 'Tapp' (Tony Tapper) and he wasn't a great reader or writer, worse than me, and he said, 'Oh, there's a lot of "S Moors" in tonight, isn't there?'

I retorted, 'It's short for Spennymoor, you daft bastard!'

I hit this lad with a thumping right and, as he went back, the book fell on his knee.

'You've dropped my book now,' I seethed.

I broke his jaw. He was with a lad called Tommy. Tommy was about 40 and he was one of the best fighters. Although I think he may have been past his sell-by date, I ran a fast cluster of five or six hooks to his body and with each shot that landed I could hear his ribs cracking as I broke them, and then I threw him unconscious down the little steps.

Tommy grassed me up to the police, the toe-rag, and I was arrested for it, but there was no proof. There was a video of it that was never given to the police; I wish I still had it but we used to wipe the tape. You could see me knocking him out in it and I wish I still had that fucking tape now. I would have made money off it: 'Big Knockouts'. There must have been about 40 or 50 knockouts on that tape where I had punched people.

I'd broken the lad's jaw in about four different places. I remember him coming back in this grey Jaguar, the old type. I ran and kicked the door, shattering the window. But, when I went to get in and drag him out, he shit himself and fucked off and I never saw him again! I found out that he was called 'The Dentist' because, when he hit you with his right hand, he would knock all your teeth out and you would have to go to the dentist the next day. This same guy has been in a few big books as the top fighter, and I destroyed him. I was 24 years old.

I had beaten everyone I had come across until I was 24 and I never stopped fighting when I was working on that door. You know how it is when you start fighting. People were throwing glasses at me.

They got the message in the end, but in those days they were calling us 'The Magnificent Seven' and people used to come along humming the tune, and the bastards used to smash our car windows all the time. Eventually the same people had respect for us and used to say, 'Fucking hell, you're a better fighter than me.'

People liked us and then we moved on to work on another few doors. I was working in Henry Africa's, where I met this girl called Christine Hilton, a big, tall, blonde lass, about five foot eight. She was lovely and we started going out.

But she had a boyfriend called Max. 'Oh, he's mental,' she said.

I don't think she knew that I was as subtle as a steamroller when it came to violence. Because I was such a nice person, and I am, she didn't know my darker side.

Christine warned, 'He's a lunatic, you know.'

Anyway, he came for her. 'Mad Max', they called him. He was in a wrecking crew. They were like a gang that got together and said, 'Let's go out on a wrecking spree and have a good time.' They would go into pubs 20- or 30-handed and the doormen would be terrified. Fuck 'em, I thought. I didn't give a fuck. I think I am a throwback to *Braveheart*, where there were only 200 of Braveheart's men against 3,000.

We were on the door and this Max came up and went over to Christine and smacked her in the face! Obviously, he had been beating her.

I sauntered up to him and blasted, 'You, you daft cunt ...'

My right hand felled him and his neck chain dropped off and he said, 'I want my chain, mate.'

I put him on his arse, knocked him out, and when he came round he was mumbling, 'I'm going to fucking kill …'

'Come on then.'

He kept walking away and eventually fucked off.

About a year later, he came back and strutted up to me in the Waterfront.

'You, you cunt,' I snapped.

I nutted him and hit him with a right uppercut and he hit the deck. With just those two shots, I broke his jaw, fractured his skull and broke his nose. Although his face looked like a burst mattress, he never grassed, so I have to give him his due.

Anyway, he fucking came back again a year later when I was working in Chaplins in Stockton with a lad called Malcolm Cook. I had been working for John, when somebody offered me a door; I got offered Chaplins and then I was offered another door, in Berlin's. So I was earning double the money that John was giving me and it was all right, so I started working on a few more doors. I wasn't making a fortune, I'm talking about £200 a week, but it was decent wages back in the 1980s.

While working in Stockton I started to live with Christine. I didn't know anybody there because I came from Redcar. We were living in her house at Roseworth, one of the housing estates. As I didn't drive, Christine taught me. To show you how much of a temper I had, I used to kick the car lights out, blaming it for not working. Christine said, 'When you drive, you drive and you don't think about it and that is when you know you are driving. It's when you are thinking about it that you start making all the silly mistakes.' Of course, she was right.

But back to the story of the wrecking crew. I had worked in the club for John and they would threaten to come in on a Sunday night. This time there were only about eight or nine of them. People would be scared of them, intimidated by their size, as a lot of them were big lads, some 15, 16 stone, but it was mainly the size of the gang.

I was in the pub and they were standing there with a menacing air. They had been upstairs and they said, 'A bottle of dog,' to Amanda, who worked there. I didn't know what this was – I thought it maybe meant brown ale – and Amanda didn't know either. They sat and argued and one of them started grabbing her. This lad named Big Ste was there and another lad was with me.

Those of you familiar with pub brawls will know that it's just a melee of madness, but that's not how I work! I am like a kid in a candy store when such things kick off with the colourful locals intent on madness. In the right situation, I can turn into the worst council-estate pit bull in a millisecond!

I was ready to go to war. I dropped two of the rogues' gallery at the back of the bar after I had used my brutal charm on them. One of the others had hold of Ste and started biting his tit, and Ste was screaming. I punched him right in the face and wiped him out, but I wasn't finished! The pit bull in me had been unleashed and I bit chunks out of him. I bit right through his fucking cheek and he soon let go, the fucking cunt.

My reign of terror wasn't over yet. I went to grab him and I elbowed him, but it was one of the pub's glass collectors ... he fell to the floor like a broken doll. I grabbed another lad, picked him up as if he was helium-filled and tossed him into the air like a pancake. He landed on this fucking table and nearly broke his back because the tables were marble-topped.

In the aftermath, the police come in. Someone had said that it was a big Pakistani that had assaulted them. I am dark-skinned with dark hair and I had a moustache then. The police were looking for an Asian gentleman.

'There's no Asian gentlemen working here, Officer' I said.

We were all right, so then they went.

Then there was another night when they came in about 15-handed; there was Ste, me and a few others. They had sneaked in and gone upstairs in ones and twos. We were downstairs in the other bar, as we weren't really working and nobody had noticed because it was a Sunday night.

Apart from the 15 upstairs, there were about 20 of them out in the street and they must have thought I was going to run.

I roared, 'Come on, you fuckers!'

This was going to be like the St Valentine's Day Massacre. I dropped about three or four of them in the street and then two others came over and I fucking sparked one; he fell on his arse.

The police came up and one of them said, 'Bloody hell! I've never seen anyone fight like that in my life. It was excellent, that.'

They had been trying to get this wrecking crew for some time and they were over the moon that I had brayed all the fuckers in the street.

After that, I was just walking through the market and I saw Mad Max there. Dark anger descended on me like a widow's veil. I toyed with him before sparking him out with a booming right.

I got another one down an alley. There are some little alleys in Stockton where you go from one end of the town to the other, and bingo ... I caught him right in one of them. You know the saying I wouldn't like to meet him down a dark alley? Well, I met the cunt in a dark alley; he saw me and started sweating bullets. He was trapped like a sardine in a can without a key! There was no escape from me. I didn't half fucking bray him and I nearly killed the cunt.

On the door of Chaplins I was working for myself. I said to them, 'You need three doormen here, two on the front and one on the back to be able to cope.'

They said, 'Is that how many you need?'

I said, 'Yes, you need three doormen. Maybe if you get four, two on the back and two on the front.'

'OK,' they said.

I said, 'I can do four.'

So I was in the club and about 15 blokes came looking for trouble because I had sorted the wrecking crew the week before.

I boomed, 'Come on, you fuckers!'

I ran out at them with the enthusiasm of an undertaker and, on seeing me rushing at them like my hair was on fire, they ran like fuck!

They all ran like kids, saying, 'We're going to get you.'

'Where do you want to fight: Stockton or Middlesbrough?' I said.

They ran right to the other end of the street and they were shitting themselves because I had brayed them that many times and I had gone round their houses and brayed them there too. They were terrified of me. I wrecked the wrecking crew, and that was the end of them.

Well, it wasn't the end, as they still went into other pubs, but they didn't do it to my pubs because I had a reputation to keep.

The publicans used to say, 'Just get Brian Cockerill and they won't come into your pub.'

I'm not primarily a doorman and, as you will see, most of this account of my career is about taxing drug dealers. But, so you know my background, I'll show you how I have no fear.

I started getting more pubs and taking on more doormen. I was working the doors in one particular licensed premises – I was about 25 or 26 – when John Black told me about Lee Duffy.

'There's a lad called Lee Duffy,' he said. 'You'll get on with him because he's a good lad, you know, Brian. Duffy can fight for fun. You would get on with him well. He's like you, he'll have a go. He's special, like you.'

It wasn't until I had a broken finger that I heard of this Duffy character, which leads me to tell you of that time.

I went to Berlin's and this lad came in and had a go but he couldn't make his fists do what his mouth had predicted. I punched him from arsehole to breakfast time and broke my finger hitting him.

I threw him out and he said, 'I'll be back.'

Give him his due, he came back, but he had about another 17 cunts with him. They came in and I was at the door with a bust finger. I needed an equaliser. There was a little piece of wood above the door, like a fire-exit sign. I pulled it out and I said, 'Here, fuck off!' as I hit him with ferocious intensity on the head with it. I dropped him into the street like the filthy bag of shit he was. But there was the slight problem of the other 17 motherfuckers and only two of us on the door.

Soon the lad fucked off and I went up the stairs and I was fighting with them all. The place was a cauldron of violence. I dropped one, dropped another and, as fast as I was dropping them, they were getting up. This was like *Night of the Living Dead II*.

Then the others were fucking jumping on me and this was going on for about seven or eight minutes.

This big one invited, 'Come on then, me and you!'

I spat, 'Come on then!'

I fucking hit him and dropped him like a filthy habit and got on top of him, and as I got on top he bit a chunk out of the skin on my face. To this day, I have got a mark from that bastard's bite.

'Oh,' I said, 'so you like biting, do you?'

I turned into a demon and bit his face off like a hyena gnawing on a bone. I ripped half his fucking face open and brayed him. The rest of the bloodthirsty rabble hit me with sticks and started fucking kicking and punching the hell out of me. They were hammering me with chairs and everything, this gang. There was a trail of destruction all around me; I was ready to go to war. So I thought, Well, I am going to give this cunt it anyway because I am going to get it nevertheless.

I got up and I was still not knocked out. But I was being bombarded with everything and my cheekbone and my nose were broken, I had holes all over my fucking head where they had been thrashing me with sticks and all that, and I'm still standing up!

Still loads of the rabble spewed out all over the place. Some of them were injured and some were hurt, but they were still coming at me because I was on my own.

When the police eventually arrived, I said, 'I just fell down the stairs.'

I never pressed charges. I was taken to hospital and got fixed up.

The next day, I went in the club and the gang came and I said, 'So you want fucking more, do you?'

I saw a samurai sword through the door, a fucking samurai.

They came about 50-strong, but they were always down the other end of the pub, which was full, and I was saying, 'Come on then, you fuckers.'

And they were all like, 'He is fucking raged, this cunt, he is fucking mental.'

I hadn't had any lads with me the night before, but now I had about 20. Mark Johnson, he is a black lad, and Ali Johnson and all of them from the Mall – their entire team of doormen – all came and helped.

I said, 'I've had enough of these cunts.'

I don't like going into people's houses, but these two cheeky cunts were the type that would, so we said, 'We'll get the cunts.'

We went round to their houses and, when they came out, we struck them with venomous brutality! At one house I went to, I shattered one of the bastards' jaws and booted him all over the garden like a football.

During the course of that day, I must have got about six of them and I battered them all over. I went to this house and, it was rumoured, we had taken a shitload of handguns and put the bastards down on the floor and threatened to kill them. The story goes that we put handguns to their heads and said, 'Come any more and we will kill you, you bastards.'

After this supposed incident, that was the end of the wrecking crew, they were finished.

With my finger broken from the wrecking-crew fight, I had this metal splint to keep it straight. It took years to heal and even now the bone is still in a funny position. It was hard to train; you couldn't hold the bar, so you couldn't do presses, you couldn't train. At this time when I was training, I weighed something like 23 stone from power lifting. I was going to go for the title of the World's Strongest Man, but I didn't know how to do the events and I was probably one of the strongest people in the world at that time. I remember watching *The World's Strongest Man* on TV and the event they did was a shoulder-press. I had beaten them in the gym on the shoulder-press unofficially by four repetitions, so I would have been one of the world's strongest men.

I didn't have an agent. I just used to train in the gym and I was squatting eight-and-a-half 20-kilo plates per side of the bar and I could bench-press 630 pounds for ten reps with it. Hundreds of people have seen me do it.

I had squatted 700 pounds – not a full squat to the bottom, just a half-squat – and I was shoulder-pressing four plates. I was just phenomenally strong and phenomenally big and I still did a bit of boxing.

A lad from Eston who worked for me on the door – Mickey Mallam, I think his name was – got a door job for me at Chaplins and I was working other doors too. Anyway, Mickey had a fight with this lad called Brian Robson. I remember his name as it was the same as the footballer. Mickey punched him and the shit was about to hit the fan.

Mickey had been to jail before for punching another lad. He had hit him awkwardly and injured his neck, snapped something, and that had given him an embolism or something and he had died.

Now he had done the same thing to this lad.

I said, 'You can't fucking run, you're not going to go anywhere. They know it's you, you're on CCTV camera.'

I took him to my solicitor who advised him that, because it was a fair fight and the lad had caused the trouble, it wasn't as bad as he thought. Of course, Mickey was sent to jail after he pleaded guilty.

Not wanting to feel left out, I have been up for many charges and bailed for racketeering, blackmail, kidnapping, attempted murder, murder charges, firearms, armed robberies, section-18 woundings.

They wanted to get me behind bars for 20-year terms, so they didn't bother too much about the low-key charges. I don't know how many times they could have done me and got me two or three years behind bars. They would have, but they were going for 20-year sentences, and 15s and 10s, and the charges would be massively exaggerated.

I have been arrested for having people shot, but nothing was proven. Once I was up for a charge and my solicitor, Craig Beer, from Redcar, came in and said it was for racketeering, blackmail and kidnapping. That was what they were saying, but it was all shit and they had no proof. They are out there now, half a dozen of them, all looking through law books trying to find anything to hold you on. That is how much they hate you and want you.

To get back to Mickey's story, he went to jail and I went to see him with a lad called Kevin Kilty, a friend of mine from Winny Banks. We sat there, looked after him and talked to him, telling him everything that was going on and that everything should be all right in court. It was a fair fight, the other lad caused the trouble and there were other people there.

After seeing Mickey, Kevin and I went to this little restaurant in Redcar called the Acropolis. Afterwards, we were just leaving when we saw this Lee Duffy character driving by in a car.

I thought he seemed all right because John had said he was. We were going to see this lad called Jimmy, so we were going along the street and Lee Duffy must have been going to see the same lad, because Jimmy was a drug dealer, although we knew him through his brother, Tony Stubbs, who used to work for me. Anyway, there was Lee Duffy and he got out of the car and he had a lad called John Fail in tow.

I didn't know these people from Adam, but we didn't want to cause trouble for Jimmy, so we started to walk back to Kevin's car. I heard a whistle from Duffy and I turned round.

The clash of the titans was about to explode all over the streets of Redcar!

7 THE DUFFER VS THE TAX MAN

Lee Paul Duffy	**Brian Cockerill**
Weight: 245lb	**Weight:** 330lb
Height: 6ft 4in	**Height:** 6ft 3in
Age: 26	**Age:** 25
Job: Taxing drug dealers	**Job:** Trainee in taxation
Background: Violence	**Background:** Violence
Attempts on his life: Numerous	**Attempts on his life:** Numerous
To date: Killed 25 August 1991	**To date:** Runs own security company

LEE DUFFY AND John Fail, looking like a drunken buffoon, were guzzling on bottles of Pils. Duffy had put his bottle down.

I was about 25, gullible and I wasn't into fucking sneaky tricks: I was just into straight fighting. 'The Duffer', who had caught my attention by whistling, drawled in his inimitable style, 'Now then, now then, now then, what do they call you then?'

I thought he was going to say something like, 'Hi, I'm Lee, John's told me all about you.'

Anyway, I blasted, 'I'm Brian.'

I was keeping a close eye on Duffy's mate, who by now was holding his bottle menacingly. Fatally, I played Duffy's game because, when I glanced at his mate for a split second, the Duffer caught me with a right hand that nearly took me apart! With deadly accuracy, a power-packed punch landed right on my granite-like chin. For the first time in my life, I was put into a squat position, on my arse, and I had to cover up.

I had felt the venomous power and I knew then what people meant when they said you could see stars. Everything was going black and then there were little flashes. I was seeing more stars than Patrick Moore!

Obviously, Duffy thought that this clever punch had put me out for the count, but I'm no ordinary man! I wasn't going to be the walkover that he was used to bashing up in pubs, clubs and blues parties.

I quickly shook it off and I grabbed the Duffer around the legs in a bone-crushing clasp. He tried desperately to push me away but he didn't have the strength.

My head was beginning to clear of the red mists of semi-consciousness and, while he was still in my arms, I took an almighty swing that smashed him into the wall like a champagne bottle christening a new ship.

Turning up the heat and growling, 'Let's put the show on,' I let loose a volley of headbutts that exploded on to his head like a jackhammer. I could see the word 'mug' written on his forehead as the blood trickled down, and then I crashed into him with my forearm and he dropped to the ground in an insensible heap.

So I picked him up and nutted him and then threw him a bit more. But, with my finger broken, I couldn't bend the right hand, so I half pulled him to the left and pushed him back and nutted him twice, pulled him down and kneed him in the chest and twice in the face and he fell to the floor once more.

I was on top of him and I had him with my left hand and was pinning him down with my knee, but I couldn't make a fist to punch him in the face with my right hand, so I was going to bite his face. He was shouting, 'John, John, get him off me!'

I continued laying headbutts into him even on the ground and he was screaming even louder at his beer-swilling pal, 'Failey, get him off me.'

When you've got 23 stone sitting on you, you've no chance, not unless you've a mate standing nearby with a bottle of Pils!

The Duffer was beaten, but his mate knew only one way to win, or so he thought! All I heard was the sound of breaking glass as the bottle disintegrated on my head!

My pal Kevin went, 'Here, one-to-one!'

I exploded in a fit of anger, grabbed Fail and threw him into the car. Duffy was lying defenceless on the floor, fucked! Kevin was wary of them because he knew them well; they knew where he lived. I'm not saying that he was shitting himself, because he wasn't, but he wasn't daft.

I was thinking, If I can get to my mate Mickey Stone's on the corner. Mickey was a big lad of 15 stone who could fight and he had already had a run-in with Duffy and wasn't scared, although I am not saying he would have beaten Lee Duffy.

At this stage in my life, I was quiet and didn't really want any trouble. This was in sharp contrast to the Duffer, who was a high-profile figure. I had just beaten one of the hardest men around; he'd obviously assumed I was a real underdog.

Trying to get to Mickey's, I went along the street and, as I crossed over, I could hear the Duffer and his pal running up behind me. He didn't give up easily! By now the two of them were wanting to fight me at once.

I was thinking that, by the time I beat fucking one, especially with my finger broken, the other one would be at me.

I said, 'Look, fight me when my hand is better. I will fight you.

Fucking John Black will arrange the fight. I will come and fight you when I feel better. Just wait until this hand is better and I will come and fight you whenever you want.'

'Well, I'll just drop you,' Duffy retorted.

At this I bragged, 'I just had you and you were screaming like a fucking baby: "John, get him off me, get him off me, John."'

'Just get him, Lee,' Failey was goading.

Duffy started jumping about, so I started jumping about too, like a boxer.

He went, 'Whoa!' as if to say, fucking hell, he can box as well.

I could tell his bottle had gone and in his mind he was thinking I knew how to fight. As I was dancing about, he knew the fucking score. Then I used my strength to heave on a bollard and it moved, so I gave one final yank and managed to pull it, like a rotten tooth, out of the ground.

With my makeshift weapon, I ran at Lee and he tried to smash it aside with his hand but fell to the floor. He said to Failey, 'I am going to fucking do this lad.'

I took off along an alley that ran by Mickey's house and I went into his place. But Duffy, with renewed vigour, came running to the end of the passageway and shouted, 'Come on down the alley, because I want a fight.'

'Come on then, one-to-one!' I shouted back.

We started bawling at each other, but, by the time I came out of Mickey's, he had gone.

I met up with Kevin again and he said, 'You had him beat!'

My hand was fucked, so I trained with Mark Johnson, who asked, 'Who have you had a fight with?'

'Lee Duffy,' I said.

Mark and Duffy had had a one-to-one. Duffy beat him, but Mark did have the balls to fight him – one of the only people who had the guts to do it.

I trained for about ten weeks until my hand was partially healed and I went searching for Duffy. In the meantime, I met this lad called Rick Marsen and some others: Dave Williams, Kevin O'Keefe, who was known as Beefy, Paul Brians and I think maybe Dave Williams's brother, Mark Williams, was there. There was Mickey Stone too. All top fighters, they went looking for Lee Duffy.

They were in the pool hall when Lee Duffy walked in. George Fawcett was there and Duffy said to him, 'Are you with them?'

He said, 'No, I'm going to the car, they have got nothing to do with me.'

In reality, he was with the six or seven of them who were looking for Duffy.

One of them had this sawn-off shotgun and he said, 'I'll fucking shoot you, Duffy. I'll shoot you!'

As calm as a cucumber, Lee went, 'Well, shoot me, shoot me, you daft cunt. You're all sat there; you haven't got the heart to shoot me. You shoot me and you go to jail. You are a shithouse. I'm going to bray every one of you!'

They all shit themselves and fucked off. Later Mickey Storm phoned me and I met them.

'If you fight him, we'll give you money,' they said.

'Well, I'm not scared. I'll fight him,' I told them.

All of them were so frightened of him; obviously, I wasn't that streetwise then. I wasn't that brilliant because I wasn't on the street, I wasn't doing anything. They were using me in a way, because I was babysitting them all fucking night and I never got a penny off the cunts. They were selling drugs and making fortunes.

Later, Lee Duffy said to me, 'I knew you would work them out,' because he was clever, very street savvy; he had done armed robberies and he had been to jail. When you go to jail you have got to be streetwise or you get fucking eaten alive, and he was very, very clever.

I remember this lad saying to me, 'We were working on this door and Duffy came up and said to one of the doormen, "Can you get me a job?" Duffy was only 16 and was told by the doorman, "If you can beat me in a fight, then you can have my job," and Duffy brayed him all over and he got the job and that is how he started working on the doors at 16.'

When you think of it, it is phenomenal that a kid of 16 could be working on the doors. He was really a big lad already, but he didn't grow much more until he was 26. He was one of those people who mature early and are still not much bigger ten years later. I, on the other hand, just kept getting bigger and bigger. When I was 16, I was only 10 or 11 stone.

Back to the search for Duffy. I had gone to a house where I knew he hung out. I knocked on the door and said, 'Is Lee Duffy in there?'

'No,' was the guarded reply.

'Well, tell him I'm looking for him,' I said. 'I'll fight him any time.'

I left it and went down the town, where I met this lad I know as Gunner and asked him, 'Have you seen Lee Duffy?'

He announced, 'He's just battered a lad called Peter Wilson and has broken his neck. He hit him with a punch and broke his neck and he has been remanded.'

I thought, Fucking hell! I realised Duffy had loads of people around him connected to drugs and I thought, Where does he tax his fucking deals?

With a lad called Miller, I started going round to all these fucking dealers and taxing them, just like Duffy had done.

One of our first targets was a dealer called Nipper, who dealt from a phone box. After looking for him all day, we grabbed him. He had £700 on him, which would be worth a couple of grand now.

We would tax a few and make maybe three grand in one day. I thought, Fucking hell, this is brilliant! I have made three grand.

Meanwhile, Duffy was in jail and I remember somebody saying, 'Lee Duffy is up at court.'

I went down to the court to seek Duffy out and have a fight with him. I asked my solicitor at the time, 'If I had a fight in the court here, what would happen?'

He warned me I could get nicked for fighting in a public place.

I responded with joy, 'Right, that's it! I'm going to fucking bray the cunt.'

I knew what I was going to do. If I was at the top of the stairs, like you see in the old films, I'd have the height.

After waiting and waiting, I left the court building.

Before going into court, I had noticed a car nearby with someone inside staring at me. We were walking up the street looking at this first-class prat in the car; he was wearing a pair of those big, daft fucking Chips-type sunglasses.

'Who's that daft cunt in the car looking at me?' I snapped irritably. 'Who's that mong looking at?'

It was Lee Duffy and I didn't know! So, when I got inside and got talking, they said, 'He has just been and gone, Lee Duffy.'

'So that was him in the fucking car!' I said.

The next day, Nipper's younger brother took us in the car and Mark Johnson was with us, sharing the driving. We were looking for Duffy all over fucking Eston, trawling the streets for him for hours.

Then we spotted a tatty, green, A-reg Ford Sierra and Mark said, 'There he is, Lee Duffy.'

I ordered, 'Ram the fucking car, ram the car!'

He cried out, 'I daren't, it's Lee Duffy.'

'We've been looking for him all day, you daft cunt,' I raged.

He was scared, so I had to get out of the car and run 20 yards up the road to get to Duffy; remember, I was 23 stone then. I dived on to the back of the Sierra and the engine stalled. I pulled the window wiper off, kicked the back lights out and tried to get inside, but they locked the door and drove off.

Mark said, 'You've won the fight without having a fight. You've won because he fucking shit himself.'

Yeah, not as much as you did when I asked you to ram his car, I thought to myself.

I met Peter Hoe and we talked in one of the nightclubs in Redcar. He was a nice lad, a friend of mine, and the best fighter in Eston. Peter said, 'Can you do me a favour when you tackle Lee? Make sure his foot is better because he's been shot in the foot.'

I replied, 'Did he give me a fucking chance when I had a broken hand?'

'Yeah, you're right there,' he said.

I remember going to Grangetown with Mark Miller, and I met another bloke, Trevor Thermold, who owned a pub in that area. We got talking and doing a bit of business and this, that and the other, talking and having a drink. There was a phone call for me. I don't know how I knew, but I said, 'It's Lee Duffy, that is.'

I took the phone and Duffy said, 'Look, we need to sort this out.'

I thought he meant me and him having a one-to-one, so I said, 'Any fucking time you want.'

Somebody said, 'He's outside in the car with a couple of lads!'

I used to take my training bag all over with me because I didn't drive, and I used to put it in people's cars. Well, I had the bag with me and, at first, Duffy thought I had a shotgun in the thing. Paranoia or what?

He said, 'No, Brian, you're one of the best fighters. I am one of the best fighters. All these people are winding me up, saying that one of us is going to get killed, one of us is going to go to jail or something, and it is not right. Can I come and see you or can you come and see me?' Then he said, 'Send Miller out, that shithouse!'

I sent Mark Miller out and he saw him and said, 'I want to meet Brian tomorrow in South Bank.'

Now you would think this was a set-up, but then nothing bothered me – nothing.

Later, I said to Christine, 'I'm going to see this Lee Duffy to sort it out.'

She drove us to Grangetown. I don't think Miller could drive.

I went into the house – I think it was Lee's mum's place – and he was sitting there in a chair. His mum was in the kitchen and Lisa Stockell, his girlfriend, was there. I didn't know her then but I got to know her later on. Lee was putting his shoes on his massive feet. My feet are only small.

He looked up at me and he went, 'Fucking hell, I must be mental for trying to fight him. Look at the size of this cunt!' Then he said, 'Lisa, this is Brian.'

I sat down in the chair and, fucking hell, I filled it. A moment later Mark Miller was there and he sat down and then Mark's mate Neil Booth came in.

'What the fuck's going on here?' Boothy said. 'I thought you two were fighting.'

We were all right and then Lee said, 'We'll go and get a car.'

So we went out and he got this car off a lad in Eston. He didn't even fucking know him, just took it off him. I think it was a black Orion. 'We'll drop it back later,' he just said.

Thankful for not being knocked out, the lad said, 'All right, Lee, no problems.'

We were off to Redcar on our first joint taxing venture. We were calling on this lad who had ingeniously designed a lethal killing device made from a bowling ball. After drilling out holes on the ball, he had pushed deadly sharp nails into the holes, point outwards. The ball was suspended above his door on a piece of steel wire. Any unsuspecting victim walking in and being hit with such a lethal weapon would be caused some problems. He wouldn't be able to play the harmonica again, and more likely be killed.

They were going to set it to hit any nefarious character setting foot in the door. This was the plan, the lad was telling everyone. I was mentally alert when I spotted him. I cagily knocked on his door, he came out and I fucking grabbed him, which took some of the steam out of him. It hurts to get hit on the leg by a 330-pound guy with a hammer – especially when it's me on the other end of the hammer.

When the cunt tried to hit me in the face with a snooker ball, hand-to-hand combat became hammer-to-kneecap combat.

I told him, 'I'll fucking smash your fucking head in, you cunt.' So he was whacked again with the hammer in the other kneecap, which elicited screaming that would have made a banshee proud. By the time I'd finished he had more hits than Elton John. I mean, most drug dealers lead a wretched existence, selling drugs in the hope of making their fortunes, so this was no different.

'I want some fucking money now, you cunt,' I demanded.

'I've only got a grand,' he croaked, as I dragged him into the house, which was far off being the swanky house on the hill that most drug dealers hope to have one day. Outside it was absolutely pissing down, and when you walked you got soaking wet. As I dragged the destroyer of a thousand lost souls along the floor, my boots were squelching from the rain. Must get a new pair of boots, I thought.

From his stash, he managed to pull a small wad of money, so we got 300 quid apiece: three for me, three for Lee and three for Mark. All for ten fucking seconds of work, which was better than a poke in the eye with a stick. I took to it like onions take to soup.

While we were down there we got this other lad, another cheeky cunt, a horrible cunt, who was selling drugs to the kids.

The dealers had created a monster in me because they made a mint from pickling people's souls!

We grabbed this piece of filth and tossed him into the boot and took him down the Gare in Redcar. The Gare is a road a couple of miles long that goes down to a pier where they fish. At the end, there's a 15-foot drop into the water.

We got the drug-dealing cunt, put a bag over his head, tied his hands together and he still wouldn't tell me where his stash was. We tied his feet and his hands, put a rope around him and threw him in the fucking sea. We left him in there for about four or five seconds and pulled the cunt in like a fish.

'Where is the fucking stash?' I said.

He told me every fucking thing then, so we got the stash, about four grand, off the cunt. It was hidden under the floorboards and he had some blow, cannabis resin, which Lee took because he smoked it. Call Lee hypocritical, but this wasn't class-A shit.

He said, 'There's a bit for you,' as he handed me some.

He left about 20 quid's worth for the dealer and said, 'There's a bit of blow for you.'

'Thanks very much, Lee,' he said.

We had just taken four grand from him and here he was thanking Lee!

We were running about and making money, but at this particular time Lee was banned from going into Teesside as part of his bail conditions relating to the incident with Pete Wilson, so we went over Guisborough way.

On the Saturday night, we went to the Belmont, Freddy Vasey's pub. I said I was Brian Cockerill and we were introduced to all the Middlesbrough people that we were sitting with. People were beginning to realise who I was; they knew that I'd had a fight with Lee.

At the Havana club in Middlesbrough, Lee reached out his hand and offered me a fucking little half a tablet.

'What is it?' I asked.

'Just have half, you'll be all right,' he told me.

I was 26 and I'd never had a drug in my life. He gave me this biscuit; it was called ecstasy. I didn't know what it was and the next moment I was all fucking cabbaged! I didn't know where I was at and I thought, Fucking hell, I've got to sit down. So I went to the car and Lee was like a fucking lunatic, jumping about, while I was sitting there fucking monged. I was watching him and he was looking at me dead concerned and looking after me.

I was absolutely cabbaged. Lee shook my hand and said he would never fight me again, like you do when you are kids. If he'd wanted to, he could have taken a liberty, like he had with other people in the past, and brayed me all over. No, he perhaps thought, but I don't even think it crossed his mind.

He said, 'This lad, here, this lad would stand with you and die with you.' That is what he used to say to Mark Hartley and people like that. He used to say, 'See the big fella, he would stand with you and die with you.'

We met a lad called Terry Dicko. He was only little and he was mad, doing all these kicks and dancing and jumping about and having a bit of a laugh. Lee said to him, 'Here, he is the best fighter I have ever met in my life. He beat me that day, you know. There's nobody can beat him.' Lee was saying that to Terry and people in the pub, and, 'He is the best, he is the real deal in boxing terms.'

I'll give Lee Duffy his due: later on, when we got to be friends, he said, 'That day you beat me was the first time in my life I had been beaten and I couldn't sleep for weeks on end thinking there's someone better than me in Teesside.'

8 THE HOTTER THE FLAME, THE QUICKER THE BURN

LEE AND I were in this little car, a Fiat Punto, driving about all over and I was 23 stone and he was about 17, 18 stone, and we were fucking stuck together.

I gasped, 'Move over, you big cunt, I'm monged.'

Lee went off to the Belmont, but I was just too fucked from this half a tablet he had given me. I thought it was a vitamin pill, that's how green I was! Sitting there, it just seemed like I was in the car for hours; it just went on for ever, this feeling. But then all of a sudden I was all right and jumping about.

Later, we hunted down this drug dealer called Dave the Rave. He had some pretty fish in a tank and I was playing with them as I was saying, 'I'm going to fucking stab you! I want your fucking money.'

Anyway, we took about 600 quid off him. Lee fucked off and I didn't see him for about two days. He went to Newcastle, I think. I went out with TJ, Mono from South Bank [in Middlesbrough] and a few other lads, about six of us. I had all the money on me, so I took them out for the day to Redcar and we all started to have a drink. Although I didn't drink, I let my hair down and I was fucking drunk.

Outside the pub, they were saying, 'Show us your strength!'

I was picking cars up off the ground. The bumpers were made of metal then, but you were OK as long as you had a beer mat, or a T-shirt, that you could put under the bumper to save the metal cutting into your hands. They were easy to lift, but I remember once, being the show-off, I nearly sliced off my finger and that was a horrible feeling. Try that stunt now and the bumper would come off with half the car attached to it! I tried to do it when a woman got her wheel stuck down a drain or manhole cover that had broken. I pulled at it and half the fucking wing came off. Cars are rubbish now.

We were running about in Redcar and word got back that the bouncers had brayed big fucking Norman, who is about 16 or 17 stone. Then I ran into a lad called Ste, who was about 20 stone. I said, 'Come on, you cunt.'

I was like a mad mullah. I dropped two of the doormen and then they shit themselves and ran away. The police came and grabbed hold of me, I turned around and this lad punched me in the face while I was being held. I lost it, I was in a snarling mood. I threw the police out of the way and started trying to get hold of the lad. They were trying for ages to put me in the van and in the end they succeeded. In the chaos and darkness inside, I kicked the hinges right off the doors and the doors flew off like autumn leaves.

They put me in another van, so I said, 'Go on, put me in another one, I'll just kick them off again. You can't do anything about keeping me in the van!'

This copper came up to me and said, 'Look! You're going to get yourself loads of shit and some big compensation orders if you keep doing this!'

So I went in the other van and later got nicked for criminal damage and for assault on the lad. When I went to court, I got bail, but I didn't prefer charges against the lad that cracked me in the jaw while the police had hold of me. It wasn't in my fucking character, so I got done for criminal damage and resisting arrest. Eventually I was found guilty of criminal damage and given a £1,100 fine.

About three nights later, we were driving through Eston and I said to Lee, 'There's that fucker who fucking attacked me the other night.'

He stood there as hard as nails in this kebab shop.

I said, 'Run at me.'

He was a first-class-honours nutcase. He ran at me and I caught him with a cast-iron right uppercut that lifted him right off his feet. His jaw came apart in three places and he went sprawling to the ground. He was awake but technically knocked out.

'Fucking hell, he's gone grey!' I said.

He'd gone from brown to grey in seconds; his body-builder's tan had faded. All these body-builders train their muscles and look good, but you can't train your fucking chin; you have got to learn how to fight. You can't just walk about looking big. Because when it comes to the nitty-gritty you find yourself in deep shit! In the crucible of my early years, I was always top dog. I could use my size and strength until I gained my street skills.

The hotter the flame, the quicker the burn, they say, but it isn't always true! A lot of people would say, 'I wouldn't like to fight him, he's 20 stone!' But you can get lads that are 10 or 11 stone who can beat people at 20 stone and keep going.

Anyway, this fucking muppet drug dealer grassed me up to the police; he made a statement straight away. Lee and I were running about and the next minute the police had nicked me.

The copper who pulled me in said, 'We're getting over 100

phone calls a week about you and Lee Duffy kidnapping people, kicking doors in, taxing drug dealers and taking money off them. We're not fucking bothered because they're only scumbags anyway, but we have got to do something about it, because we have got ranks.' This copper was all right with me, not nasty or anything.

Just before I got nicked, Mark Miller's sister brought her boyfriend round to stay for the night. In the middle of the night, the boyfriend decided to help himself to the telly and video and she caught him going out of the door with them. He also punched his sister and bust her eye. We were nicked because we were supposed to have kidnapped him, taken all his clothes off him, driven him up to a place called Thorpe field and brayed the cunt, then thrown him out of the car and made him walk home with a pair of underpants on. Apparently, he went to a nearby house and they phoned the police for him. I was at Christine's at Roseworth when I was nicked. Miller got arrested at his house and was remanded to prison.

I was in the house and I had a dog called Ben, a big Rottweiler that weighed 14 ½ stone – a fucking huge dog! I remember Stevie Sayers coming to my house one night after he had been to a rave.

I said, 'Come on in, the dog is all right. Have you seen my dog?'

'Oh, bring it in,' he said.

He was sitting on the settee and he thought I was going to bring in this little dog, but when he saw it he yelled, 'Fucking hell, Brian, get that fucking monster out of here!'

There was a threatening knock on the door, followed by, 'Are you in the house? This is the police.'

This was about two o'clock in the morning. All the neighbours must have been sick to death of living near me. The police got into my back garden, so I let the dog out and he ran at them and they all fucking shit themselves and went racing down the alley. I ran out of the back and dived over the fence. I was lying down beside the fence as they searched the house.

Eventually the police switched their search to the gardens, shining their torches like there was no tomorrow. I was there on the ground and they were standing looking for me with their torches blazing.

One of them said forlornly, 'I don't know, he must have got away, because he's never come back in.'

Just before this, I had to take the dog back in because the police were around the back of the house. They were not more than three feet away from me as I lay hidden beside this fence – all 23 stone of me! It happens, doesn't it? You can walk past somebody and not realise they are there. How can you sneak a man my size over a fence? I couldn't get over it and into the street, so I just lay in the grass until they assumed I must have gone. Then I sneaked back into the house and went back to bed and Mark got remanded for a week.

The lad was kidnapped again and I was eventually nicked outside Frankie Atherton's house in Redcar for kidnapping.

The police were glowing when they said, 'We've got you this time, Cockerill. You are going to get 15 years for this.'

Within two hours, the lad came into the police station and said, 'Brian Cockerill never kidnapped me. I was just off my head and they were helping me.'

All the charges were dropped and the police were devastated once again.

I was back on the road with Lee Duffy and we had 600 quid that day. The same day, in Gateshead, Lee met this lad called Craig Howard that he knew and got this charley [cocaine]. We went to a house with him. People there were on this coke, sniffing the stuff, and they were talking to me and they were laughing.

Lee said to me, 'You know that fucking fight we had?'

Here we go, I thought. 'Oh, forget the fight, Lee,' I said.

We were sitting in the kitchen and Craig was standing at the sink. Lee wouldn't let it go. This is his account of the fight we had: 'Well, that day you beat me, you know. For the first time in my life I had been beat and I couldn't sleep.' And he went on, 'Your fucking power is unbelievable. You know how I got him, Craig? I hit him, I dropped him. I admit I dropped him. I thought, in the finish, I was confident as fuck, and he gets up, so I dropped him again. He was up like fucking lightning, so I grabbed him by the legs thinking, I'll throw him on the floor and beat him, but he kept headbutting, elbowing and kneeing me in the face.

'I was on the floor and I thought, Fucking hell, and then when I saw him jumping about boxing, I knew he could fight.'

That's when I knew that I was thinking during the fight was true. He was thinking, Fucking hell, he can fight and he can move with his feet and he can box and he can do all these things. He said he was just jumping about thinking, I have got to look good here in front of other people. Well, he knew that I was powerful, but he had had me on my arse and it was the first time I had ever seen stars.

He said, 'I don't think anybody can beat you in the country, the fucking what do you call him, down London, the governors and all them, none of them would beat you, and they are the best.'

When the Duffer liked you, I think he really liked you.

Then he said, 'Come and show Craig how fast you are.'

There were some boxing mitts and pads lying about in the house, and Craig said, 'How can you be that fast, your hands beat the laws of physics? You can't be that big and that fast at the same time.'

Then Lee was on pads and then I was holding the pads, and I was wondering if he was going to slide a sly one with the pads – you know, when daft things go on in your head – but he didn't and he swore on his kids' life in the kitchen that he would never

76

do anything sneaky or hit me on the sly. 'You are my friend for life,' he swore.

I used to say to Lee, 'You shouldn't go into pubs fucking punching people. Fair enough, have the first one on the cheek, fucking give them it, but don't let anybody take the piss out of you. But at the end of the day, it wouldn't be nice walking in a pub. And people would come to like you and be friends and stay there. Because one day those people who you are hitting will become men and you'll become an old man or you might need help.' I went on, 'They don't help you because you've done bad things to them.'

I think he used to sit and listen to me and he used to say, 'You speak a lot of sense, you do, big fella. A lot of people just use me and I'll jump in to help people and I do daft things.'

I will always remember Lee as being kind-hearted. I remember him having a £400 jacket and one of the lads said, 'Oh, I like that jacket, Lee.'

He said, 'Here, man, just have it.'

I didn't know a lot about taxing. I only knew a little bit about Lee's deals, but somebody told me he got about 10, 15, 20 grand at a time. Lee loved to let everyone in on what he was doing. The police and everyone knew what he was doing; he couldn't keep anything a secret.

The more time passed, the more I became involved in taxing the dealers. I think it started with Lee because he would give every fucker gear and they all ripped him off. He couldn't control any of them, so he started taxing every fucker. He said, 'Fuck it, I've just spent ten grand there and I've only got seven grand back!'

After he started taxing them, he was better off for taxing the cunts and taking the drugs and the money off them and there was no chance of getting caught. Then, cleverly, he would set things up and we would go all over at night. Admittedly, we did a few grand from the dealers, but my stance with the drug dealers was a tougher one than when I was with Lee. I detested them earning from the pickled souls they cabbaged!

Compared to what I was to go on to do, Lee's deals were the tip of the iceberg! More than once, I've had 50 grand, 100 grand and amounts like that. We have had people who have said to potential dealers, 'I've got two kilos of charley, it's excellent.'

You might get someone to give them a bit of charley, but the rest didn't exist! I remember one lad, only about three or four years ago, was selling heroin. He was fucking big in the clubs at that time, but he couldn't get any of the stuff.

I said, 'I can get you some, but it's 22.' That meant £22 grand a kilo.

So what I did is I got a bag of Silver Spoon sugar and I put a black bag around it, and I rolled clear sticky tape around and around and I dipped it in a bit of diesel so that it had that authentic smuggled smell about it.

I said, 'You'll have to come over because it stinks a little bit.'

He said, 'I'll send a taxi driver.'

I said, 'Well, I want that money.'

He gave the lad who went to pick up the money 17 grand. Liam and I each got eight grand and we gave a grand to the lad.

The taxi driver who picked the gear up blurted, 'If I get caught for this, I'll get jail!'

What he didn't know was, it was only a two-pound bag of sugar!

When the dealer opened it up and found out it was sugar he phoned me and complained, 'What the fuck is this you've sent me?'

'Here,' I said, 'that's Silver Spoon. Have two lumps on me.'

What could he do? He couldn't go to any other firm to get it back. I thought to myself, Well, it is less on the streets; if he has got nearly 20 grand to spend on drugs, then it is 20 grand's worth less on the street.

I've done some beauties. We got one who was supposed to be selling ecstasy and we learned he had 36 grand in the house. They called him 'Cockney Mark' and he was about six foot five and weighed about 25 stone; a big fat lad. A lot of people know him around here, but he was staying with somebody in Sunderland and he had left his coat or something in the lad's house and the lad found a number in the jacket pocket. They phoned the number and it was a police inspector on the other end of the phone!

It didn't take long to work out this grass's place in the scheme of things. It turned out that this Mark had been caught with 100 kilos of blow and he was bailed on the strength of what he promised to do for the police in setting up other dealers. He was allowed to carry so much of these drugs, getting into the villains in different areas, fucking letting the police know and they, the police, were maybe giving him ten kilos or something, which he was selling to the dealers and the police were nicking them from their honey trap, trapping them with the gear.

I found out about Mark's set-ups, so I took some tax off the fat cunt. I went into this house in Hartlepool, there were a few other lads with me, and we said, 'We've got guns.'

There was a big London firm with him and, when we went in, there was a cockney with him, a big lad called Billy, and he thought he was the bee's knees, running about with this scumbag, and that he was the best fighter. I remember him trying to stop my girlfriend Christine, the one I used to live with. He stopped her at the door in Billingham and demanded, 'You'll have to pay. You're Brian Cockerill's lass, so you will have to pay double, won't you?'

He thought he was a clever cunt. I am one of these people who never forgets anything. I have got a memory like an elephant. When I kicked the door in and went into the house, this big fat cunt came at me and I gave him a crash course in manners by sending him to the dead zone with a vicious, corkscrew right hand.

There was this other bright-looking spark sitting there, looking a bit too cute; he was about 17 stone and about six-two. Boom! I picked him off with a slick left hook.

As this happened so quickly, the cockney was still falling, and he fell on the settee, and hit the other one and he in turn fell on the floor. I turned around and there was the one called Billy.

I said, 'Who are you?'

He stuttered, 'I, I, I'm just from London. I'm just visiting.'

I said, 'Well, fucking shut up and keep an eye on the floor show.'

They were sitting there shitting themselves. I feasted my eyes on the money and took 36 grand off them. We were supposed to be there selling ecstasy and the next minute, I had this bag of fucking money! There were no Es; it was all bullshit.

When I hit this fucking lad, I knew it was fat Cockney Mark.

'What do they call you?' I asked.

He put his hands up in a defensive gesture and said, 'Brian, Brian, please, don't hit me.'

I thought he was calling out my name and meaning for me not to hit him.

I said, 'What's your fucking name?'

Again he went, 'Brian.'

He was saying his name was 'Brian'. I was losing it and I shouted, 'Brian fucking what?'

He broke down crying and bawled, 'Brian.'

I lost the plot and snapped, 'I'll fucking kill you, you cunt.'

I brayed him and he was screaming like a fucking guinea pig, I fucking battered him all over the house and took his money off him and that was it and he was the best fighter in Billingham.

I didn't give a shit who they were or what firm they were. Lee was the same; he didn't give a fuck who they were. We didn't give a shit if it was Don Corleone's gear, we would still have taken it.

What we used to do is hit a place, say Redcar, but you would only get two or three doors and everybody would be on the phone saying, 'They're at our house, they're doing it in.'

You would only get so much gear, drugs or money and then you would have to go to the next place. So then we would hit Eston and then we would hit Middlesbrough and then Billingham and then Thornaby. You see, Teesside is massive and, when you put all these little places together, there are loads of places to hit. If you put them all together, it is non-stop. There's always someone selling gear, isn't there?

We went to one place and, funnily enough, the lad ended up working for me. He ended up being one of my doormen.

Lee said I could open any fucking door, even a bank vault, 'He would kick it in, he was that strong.' At the gym in Stockton, I was benching 500-odd pounds and they all stopped to look. Lee was there and he was quite strong and would bench about 300 pounds. He was more like a Lennox Lewis-type of fighter, fast on his feet, moving around, and people would look at us, no matter where we went. There were people wanting to get Lee and people wanting to get me, but not the two of us. Fuck that! It was bad enough trying to take one out, never mind both of us!

Everywhere shut down, nobody was selling drugs, because we were taxing all the drugs and taxing all the money. Everyone was fucked and they had to go to Newcastle and Sunderland to get gear, we were told in the pubs. The area was like a ghost town in some places. People were just fucking scared. 'If we buy gear, they're going to take it off us or take money off us!'

No matter who they were, we didn't care. Every single day we had someone in the boot of the car; nearly every day, I would say, we were taking people's cars off them, kidnapping people, breaking their legs, breaking their hands and it was just relentless. It went on for months and months.

I will tell you a story about Eston. I went there with Lee and

Mark Miller and we kept banging on the door of this flat and I thought, Fucking hell, it's solid! It was locked solid, both sides, so I had to kick it and kick it and kick it until it snapped in half and my leg went through it.

My leg was stuck and all the alarms were ringing because we were above a doctor's and if you smashed something all the surgery's alarms went off. In that flat, they were selling more drugs than the doctor below!

'The police are coming,' the others shouted.

'Don't talk,' Lee was saying.

I was saying to the half-demolished door, 'Get off me, you cunt!'

Lee and Mark Miller ran off, and I was stuck in the door. In the end, I smashed the whole fucking door and just left a big hole, then took off in the car.

I would be the eternal optimist and say, 'Let's stay out a bit longer and get some more money.'

Mark Miller used to fucking hate it, but me and Lee were non-stop, relentless. We wouldn't give in, we were like bloodthirsty bloodhounds. We just wouldn't stop until we got more money and then we would keep going some more to the nth degree.

I remember Boogy telling me once they were on a beach somewhere, eating a fucking picnic. The next minute, they said, Lee was ready for a fight with Newcastle's Viv Graham.

They liked winding him up. He would go to these nightclubs and jump out of the back of a van shouting, 'I am the god of hellfire.' And he would punch Viv Graham's fucking doormen, saying, 'Tell your boss he's going to get that!'

He once knocked three or four of them out and the last one was told, 'I'll leave you on your feet so you can tell your boss what happened here.'

I really don't think that Viv Graham would have beaten Lee unless he had got hold of him, as Lee was too fast for him. Lee would have destroyed Viv; he was too tall and too fast. They were both brilliant fighters, but in different ways. Viv would go out with big gangs of lads whereas Lee Duffy would go on his own.

I remember Lee going to Rockshots nightclub in Newcastle on his own and he didn't give a fuck. He said his customary, 'Now then,' and just walked in and had a couple of shots, jumping about like a lunatic. 'I'll fucking chin you all,' he was saying.

He didn't give a fuck, and none of them dared say anything. The intimidating figure of Lee Duffy would have given them his Teesside stare and left a trail of destruction after destroying them – if anyone was ready to fight. They might have shot him or stabbed him; but fighting, he would have destroyed any one of them.

I never saw Lee punch a single person for nothing; I remember he slapped one lad in the gym because he said something stupid, but he never punched anyone in the three months I was working with him.

When we were taxing, what we used to do was good guy, bad guy; like good cop, bad cop. I used to get the dirty end of the stick and had to be the baddy, screaming and shouting, and I used to drop hints like bricks, 'Look, you're going to have to pay him. It's Lee Duffy and he is raged!'

Then Lee would say to them, 'Well, this cunt is fucking mental; even I can't control him, you know. I can fight but, if he kicks off, we're both battered!'

That would do the trick, and we would get money and stuff out of them. I would only take off the bad drug dealers or the pieces of shit. There were just too many drug dealers to get around, so the worst ones were high on my wanted list and I was attracted to them like a moth to a flame. I mean, there were drug dealers without scruples supplying kids on the streets and in schools! It wouldn't be a decent person working for British Steel or a decent person working in Woolworths or something like that. These were people out of the rogues' gallery, fucking robbing and doing all the things that they do.

This is not movie stuff, it's real! I'm not saying we were fucking heroes, but people would treat us like Robin Hood, robbing all the baddies, and a few times we would give to the needy. Once an old blind man was robbed and we went round and gave him a few hundred pounds and got all his stuff back. But you never hear about things like that in the papers. You only hear about all the times when the police have you arrested.

What I am saying is, if you do one bad thing, people remember that for a long time, but if you do 20, 30 good things they don't remember any of that, they only remember that he is fucking mental and he did this and that.

We started to spread our net of taxation further. We went to Stockton, to this guy Slitter's house. He was one of the wrecking crew and Duffy couldn't get him because he fucking shit himself and ran off.

At another house we knocked on the door and went in and as Lee pointed at me he said, 'Who is the best fighter out of me and him?'

This lad stood there in this big Victorian house that had huge windows with a little wall outside. I kid you not, this lad ran full pelt and dived through the window, landed over the side of the wall and ran up the street.

I said, 'Fuck it, he deserves to get away.'

It was like something out of a James Bond film. I have never seen anything like it. There were just so many funny things that went on.

I remember Lee giving a tax cut. He went to this lad's house and said, 'Where is your fucking gear?' The lad had got this blow on the carpet with a blanket covering it. Lee had taken 5,000 acid tabs off him but there was ten kilos of blow on the floor and he just kept stepping over it and didn't realise it was there. I believe it was about 25 grand's worth – not that I sold drugs or anything – and Lee didn't see it and walked off with his five grand's worth of gear.

One of the ways I would tax drug dealers was to pretend that I had drugs to sell them, say six ounces of blow or some acid. They would come with the money and I would take it off them. You could make well over £600. Fucking hell, I was only getting £200 or £300 for working on the door and it was two weeks' wages in one night. This is easy, I thought, and they're only scumbag drug dealers, so fuck them.

I started taxing these lads, Lee Duffy's people, some in Redcar, some in Eston, and I used to just knock on the door and then boot the fucking thing off its hinges. Mind, if I knew there were kids and a wife in the house, I wouldn't go in. In most cases, it's just lads selling from a safe house and afterwards they go home to their wives. But the daft cunts used to have all the money and all the drugs in one place, so you used to just take the lot.

Things have changed in recent years: there are many more dealers and it has become hard work because they only have £100 or £200 worth of coke in the house. It isn't worth the hassle, whereas years ago there would be two dealers in Redcar, two main dealers in Middlesbrough, or maybe three or four, and two or three in Hartlepool. They were big dealers, who would give their lads five grand's worth of gear and the lad would have the money.

To me, these dealers and dope fiends were the proverbial crock of gold at the end of the rainbow.

9 THE MAD AND THE UGLY

WHEN I HIT that bloke Ste, in Eston I finally got arrested outside Frankie's for assaulting the lad. They remanded me for one assault to Durham because Holme House Prison wasn't open in those days, back in 1991.

What a fucking shithole! I was put in B Wing. I didn't know how the fuckers did things, as I hadn't been to jail before. You take your clothes off in reception and you go in and you get weighed on the scales. Then you get a plate of fucking shit food and you go to your bed. You get up in the morning and you do your routine, you get your porridge, slop out – in those days you used to have a bucket to piss in.

Anyway, I was there for a while and my mate Paul Thompson, Thomo, came in; he was an ex-professional boxer, a good lad. He got palled up with me and then a few people came in that I knew. Mickey Mallam who worked on the doors for me and got sent down for manslaughter, was in there, the daft cunt. He was found guilty of the alternative charge of manslaughter as opposed to murder and got about four or five years; he did well.

He said that I had set him up. I had gone against him and all this fucking shit and I had grassed him up.

I said, 'How the hell can I grass you up when you murdered someone, you stupid cunt! You punched someone and you killed him, you went in and pleaded guilty and you got four fucking years for it, you fucking idiot!'

His head had gone with all the drugs and whatever, so he tried to attack me, this silly cunt; he tried to punch me. I grabbed him, threw him on the floor and went to bray him but the screws pulled me off him.

I was keen to get into the gym and when I went there were these two Geordie lads training. I can't recall their names as it was a long time ago now, but there was another one called Spud. And I remember Paul Ashton being there. I was curling 100 kilos on the barbell with two plates each end and then the bar itself and Paul was benching fucking less than that. I was curling more on the bar than he was benching, Paul said I was fucking awesome. They were all on about this 100 kilos. I have curled a lot more than that. But bear in mind that when you are in jail you are not eating as much. 'He is going six or seven reps with 100 kilos on there,' they were saying.

Then one of them said, 'Yeah, but you can't beat a knife!'

I said, 'Shut up, you fucking muppet!'

He said, I'm going to fucking stab you,' and I punched the cunt and dropped him. Bang! Bang! I smacked him in the face and then his mate turned around, so I smacked him as well and put him on his arse. What a fucking nightmare!

I said, 'That is a sword you've got there, you daft cunt. What are you doing with a sword in here?'

The blade was about three foot long, but, give them their due, they had pinched two big knives out of the kitchens and were going to try and stab me.

There was a screw called Robson and he said, 'Come on back to your cells, lads, until we get this sorted out.'

Back then, you were entitled to watch a video, if it had Home Office approval, every three days, but when someone was caught with contraband videos, that fucked it.

I said, 'We're entitled to a video.'

The screw replied, 'You're not getting a fucking video.'

I was livid. 'Well, fuck you!'

He said something else and I said, 'Come on then, you fucking wanker!'

On the Saturday or Sunday – I know it was a weekend – I went to the gym, came back and we had our dinner and then all of a sudden the cell door opened and there were about 30 screws outside with their MUFTI (Minimum Use of Force and Tactical Intervention) gear on.

They ordered, 'You have got to go along to the [segregation] block!'

I asked, 'What for?'

'You are going down the block,' this crazy screw started shouting, but obviously he was shitting himself, the fucking shithouse.

They hadn't got the heart to do it on their own. I remember this particular screw being there, he is still there now, a big, tall lad, and he does the weights.

I said, 'Listen, mate, I swear to God, if you come into that fucking cell, that face mask, I will punch it right through your fucking face and I will bite your fucking nose off!'

He was fucking shitting himself as he stood there with his impotent six-foot-four muscular frame. I would have had him into hospital in no time!

I said, 'Come on, you come into that fucking pad [cell], come on!'

Thomo was going, 'Behave, behave,' shouting at me, 'You're going to get more fucking jail!'

The screws, shitting themselves, were pleading, 'We don't want any trouble, we don't want any trouble.'

I came out and they are lined up, in sections, all the way from B Wing to the block: a full fucking squad. There was an air of menace about me as I inspected them as if they were soldiers. 'Get your fucking shoes cleaned, you.' I was slagging them off all the way.

Then I obliged them and went to the block, where I had to take all my clothes off. I didn't want to, but you have to. I was so annoyed I snapped, 'Here, fucking have them,' and threw my shoes at them.

They were saying, 'He's fucking mental, that cunt.' I could hear them saying outside, 'He's too dangerous' and things like that.

When I demanded, 'I want my fucking exercise,' they let me go but they took along a fucking dog, and outside there were half a dozen screws taking their exercise. All this and I was only in for supposed assault.

Out of the blue, the lads decided to run a protest to stop me getting put in the block, so they sat down in the yard, about 180 of them. There were around 30 screws there.

The lads said, 'We are not coming in until he's out of the block. He was only standing up for us over the video, he's done fuck all.'

They were steadfast in their resolve to stay out there on the sit-down strike for as long as it would take. When they had been out for about ten hours, some started coming in because they were getting hungry, people who don't really know you, but I remember Benson, a black lad from Stockton, and Brian Lancaster – he is doing life now.

The gym in Durham was on the yard and some of the lads got up on to its low roof, about ten foot high. They smashed into the gym and got weights and yelled, 'Come on, you cunts,' to the screws as they went on the roof.

Now it was serious because they had broken into the gym and had weapons, so I said, 'Look, I'll go in the yard and bring the lads in and I'll just stay in the block. I'm not fucking bothered.'

I was put in the block and screws were flying all over the place, 200 or 300, all in MUFTI gear. They were shouting, 'Lancaster, come on down.'

As the lads were coming down, they were being brayed by the MUFTI squad with sticks. The screws were breaking their arms and fucking kicking the shit out of them. From the block I could hear them being dragged in screaming and the place was awash with blood.

Ten or 12 screws would be lacing into one lad. If you saw them in the street, they would put their heads down and be off. They are like fucking shithouses, petrified.

No matter where I go, they must think I am a fucking nightmare, but I was liked by the lads there in Durham or they wouldn't have sat out in the yard.

While I was in prison on remand, this man who had brought the assault charge against me had some grief. I knew nothing about it until I was eventually freed. I was well liked and people were angry with the man, they were writing on his walls, glassing him in the pub and putting his windows through, putting paint on him, fucking torturing him.

Anyway, in the end he said, 'It wasn't Brian,' and the charges were dropped.

I remember Christine came to see me, with my mate, and they said, 'Come on, you're going home.'

'Fucking brilliant,' I gushed.

I hadn't been in jail before and, out of three months, I had done about ten weeks of that in the segregation block. I am a tall person and I have got really long arms, and in that cell I couldn't stretch them properly. When I used to put my shoes on, my head would hit the wall. The seats were made of compressed paper. There was a proper bed that was bolted down and a little tiny window.

We all faced down on to the yard and people were walking through; you were looking at them as if you were on top of the world. I used to shout, 'More tea, vicar?' and the cunts on the other side used to throw piss and shit and everything out of the windows.

I met one of the Strangeways Prison rioters at Durham, Paul something; he was one of the ones who went up on the roof. He was in jail for a long time and they said he was a nonce but he wasn't. He does cartoons and drawings. I met him in 1991, then I went back to jail in 1995 and met him again and he said, 'All right, Brian? Whenever you come in here, I meet you.'

The first thing I did after being released from remand was stand on the weighing scales. I had lost fucking three stone!

While I was on remand, Lee Duffy was killed and it was 'Tapper' Tapping that shouted up, 'Lee Duffy was killed last night. He got stabbed to death.' This was a Sunday morning and I think he was murdered on the Saturday night.

It was in April 1991 that Tapping himself was alleged to have made the third attempt on Duffy's life, when petrol was thrown over him in the Commercial pub in South Bank. Attempts to light the petrol failed and as a consequence the petrol thrower was hit and received a broken jaw. Later, Tapping was acquitted of attempted murder when witnesses failed to turn up at the trial held in May 1992. Ironically, Duffy, who was charged with GBH on Tapping immediately after the petrol incident, never stood trial.

Mind, Tapper was all right and, although Lee broke his jaw, he didn't grass him up. It was other people and the police who had wanted this.

It was on 25 August 1991 that Lee Duffy died as a result of

being stabbed by David Allison, in a fight outside a club called the Afro-West Caribbean Centre in Marton Road, Middlesbrough. Lee died on his way to hospital after a main artery was severed near his armpit. The only money he had in the world was what was found in his pocket when he died – £60.

I wasn't doing the doors any more, though I still knew all the doormen, and now I just went off the rails and started taxing every cunt. Anyone who was taxable, I taxed them. I got back to the gym and got my weight back on and I became a dark cloud over the heads of Teesside's drug dealers.

I no longer had the camaraderie of Lee Duffy. I was on my own, but I didn't need any fucker. Then I learned to drive with Christine and passed my test. I couldn't work the good-guy, bad-guy routine. I just had the mad, bad guy in me that wanted to go and traumatise the ugly, fleeing tax dealers. This was going to be the supreme mad and ugly show.

I used to infiltrate gangs by saying, 'Look, do you know such and such?' and taking it from there.

Everyone knew me because I was the best fighter, and because of the likes of Lee Duffy, God rest his soul. I had beaten the best, therefore I was the best. I was bigger and stronger than Lee and, because of my size, I was also more intimidating.

I got in with different people, like Bam Bam, who is my mate – he is doing life now for another murder – and a lad called Mark Ormsby, who is dead, God rest his soul. I was running about with Beady and people like that; I met him at a rave at a club called the Eclipse.

We went to the Eclipse when Stevie Lloyd and Don Lorosh had it and I thought, This won't fucking work. Some of the doormen that used to work for me now worked on the door there, so I started going in. I was still taxing every fucking nightmare of a dealer.

I was in the Eclipse on its first night and there were about 30 people in. It was fucking rubbish. I went to Newcastle to see the Sayers brothers, Stephen and Michael. Michael started coming down and the numbers coming into the club picked up and we started getting a couple of thousand people in. It would be open all night, right into the next day, twelve until twelve. Sometimes we would have it open for two or three days and ecstasy dealers used to come in, so I used to tax them.

At New Year, I went out for ten days in a row and had 17 fights and 17 knockouts! I battered them all, but not one of those fights was my fault.

I went into a pub in Billingham with Speedy and there was this lad behind the bar who had grassed him up and the lad started shouting at him. This was the festive period, when there would be big gangs of them and they thought they were safe because of their numbers. The odds against us would be 20 to 1 as there were only three of us: me, Speedy and another kid who was driving for us.

'Right,' I used to say. 'Fuck the numbers!'

This lad was wearing a denim jacket that made him look bigger, and he went, 'Do you know who I am?'

As I looked intently into his eyes, the red mist of madness descended upon me, but I calmly said, 'I'll knock you out, you daft cunt.'

I already had the measure of this flatliner. He could so easily be morgue material and I could so easily plaster him all over the walls, but these sorts of people usually wind up dead anyway. I would not need to kill him – just make a point!

He strutted towards me in front of all his mates; he looked an intimidating figure, but that cut no ice with me. I was as dangerous as they come! I held his gaze and when he was two steps away from me ... BANG! I showed him what I was all about. I annihilated him with my right hand and his lights went out as he hit the fruit machine and slid down to the floor.

There were about another 20 of his mates to sort out yet and I calmly invited them, 'Any fucker else want some?'

They seemed to dissolve into thin air. Shitting themselves, they all sat down, as I had just destroyed the best fighter out of this pack in Billingham.

By now, I was driving a Sierra Cosworth and I started rally driving and all that stuff. The police would pull me over about 15 or 20 times a day, every fucking single day, to see if they could catch me with anything in the car, because they knew I was taxing drug dealers. They would open the boot expecting to see someone trussed up like a New Zealand lamb. Looking for bodies in the fucking boot and suspecting this and that. This went on all the time.

But they would never come to my house because I was down for ten firearms calls. They would put their blue lights on, pull me over and wait for their pals in the Armed Response Unit. It was like the police were protecting the drug dealers. I was cleansing the area of them while the police seemed to be ensuring their safety.

I was beating people here, there and everywhere. I had gone off the rails somewhat; I make no excuses about that. I was off my head on E and not training as much and still thinking I was great. I was the king of the castle. People were telling me I was the best. To beat the best, you have got to train better than the best. Mike Tyson fought a lad called Buster Douglas, who was nowhere near his class, but Tyson hadn't trained for three or four months and he had been on the drink and going out, so he got beaten. He could have beaten Douglas, but he took that fight lightly and lost. Never underestimate your opponent, or you deserve to be knocked out by mugs, as happened to Tyson... well, knocked on his arse.

We would go to rave clubs and would have a good night.

People would be selling drugs, taking a few Es, but there was no trouble. These were ordinary, everyday people having a good time. This was not a collection of council-estate smackheads preparing to mug old grannies for their next fix.

At a pub someone could get stamped to death just having a game of dominoes, and that would be with only 20 people in there. Compare this with a rave, where there were sometimes 2,000 people yet there was no fucking trouble.

I used to say, 'There are a lot of villains in here,' but I'm not saying the club was a villains' paradise, as they were not able to get up to anything, they were just enjoying themselves. They were taking Es all night on a Friday and Saturday and that would put them in bed until Monday.

I thought, What is the problem with that? You get politicians and police saying that drugs are bad for you, but isn't alcohol bad for you and don't tens of thousands of people a year die through smoking? But no fucker bats an eyelid because that is legal and they are making billions of pounds.

In comparison with deaths from alcohol and tobacco, ecstasy kills maybe 10 or 12 people a year. Yes, it is sad, but most of the people who have died on Es and other drugs have already had heart problems or they have gone berserk on them by taking too many. More people die each year from eating salted peanuts than they do taking fucking ecstasy. Compare that to the hundreds who die worldwide from poking a fork into a live toaster. Three hundred people dead because of a slice of toast!

One night I'd been drinking Jack Daniels but I didn't really drink. I remember it was my birthday and we had been down the Down Town club. Bernie McDebit was on the door with me. Every fucking night this lad used to go by looking at me. He was about six foot five, with naturally big arms; you wouldn't have to train them, he naturally had big biceps, like George Foreman.

He used to wear this cut top and he used to look and walk by, thinking that he was the top dog.

Every night this cunt used to look at me like a piece of shit, so I said through clenched teeth, 'Who are you fucking looking at?'

He said, 'I'm fucking looking at you.'

He swaggered over and started doing this big, daft right hand. I ducked and he threw his left, so I ducked again and then I put my hands on my knees. I was bobbing and weaving, letting him throw these shots at me, but then I let a volley off into his dial. Bang! Bang! I dropped this massive lad and he fell to his knees. The coup de grace was coming. I tried slapping him but he dropped back to the floor unconscious. His jaw was gone. I phoned an ambulance and it came and took him. He never grassed me.

This lad with a face like a smacked arse came to the door of the club and said, 'You battered my mate in the mouth not long ago.'

He pulled a knife on me and tried to fucking slash me across the face! I jumped back and then forward, like Smokin' Joe Frazier. When he threw a left hook, Frazier always used to spring off his feet and catch them in shock. It's called the reebok punch, because you jump like a reebok. Tyson used to throw the same punch.

I was on the steps, so I jumped off them and knocked him out. This policewoman was nearby and she came over and arrested me, saying, 'I've just seen you hitting that lad for no reason.'

This arsewipe that I had just decked had dropped his knife and his pal had picked it up and fucked off with it when the police came.

Then the manager, Kenny Gregory, was there. 'Look, he just pulled a knife out,' he said to the short-sighted female Pc.

She said, 'There was no knife' and said to me, 'You are arrested for assault.'

Meanwhile, the arsewipe was unconscious on the floor.

Kenny said to the Pc, 'Come on, the camera was on the door.'

Then he took her upstairs and showed her and she came down and said, 'I apologise. I saw him pull the knife and saw the knife on the camera.'

They say the camera never lies. The camera certainly saved my bacon that night. I could have been locked up for three, four or five years for defending myself. It is so easy: there are loads of people in jail doing time for things they haven't done.

That night we went back to the nightclub where we had been earlier. There were about six or seven of us and, when we came out, there, waiting for us, was a 30-strong reception committee of brick-throwing louts. One of the well-aimed missiles just missed me and hit Tony Buxton, splitting his head open like a coconut. He needed 17 stitches and I think he ended up getting compensation of about 20 grand. Even now, years later, his face looks fairly bad.

Like something out of *Braveheart*, I charged at the baying mob, who were pelting me with anything they could get their hands on. I got hold of one in this garden and fucking battered him to a pulp. I didn't kill him, but there was nothing left of him, he was in a bad way! He was throwing stones and, as they say, sticks and stones … I didn't know any fear because I wasn't bothered about anybody; even gangs didn't bother me.

I went to this rave and Speedy came over and said, 'You battered them,' and this and that. He was only a little lad, about 11 stone and five foot seven, but he is one of those people that you come across that you have got to kill and put in a hole somewhere, because you could fight him all day long and he would still come back and kill you. If you come at him, you'd better bray him because, if you don't, he will come back at you with a knife. I have met people like Speedy and had to break their fingers and hands with hammers. I had to do it.

I had people behind me that were as dangerous as him, so

anyone who attacked me knew it would be like putting a gun to their head. I might get killed but so would they. Rather like a game of nuclear bombs really, because they keep the peace. So that was the scenario and we got to be good friends. He was only little, but he could fight and so he had fights with people. He was no mug and he was a highly dangerous lad.

If you said, 'Go and shoot them,' he would just go and shoot them. If you wanted him to stab them, he would go and stab them. Anyway, he started running about with me and we were doing this, that and the other. We were doing a few taxes and things, and he knew everyone in Stockton, because he had lived there all his life, and he came from a rough area. We used to go to raves and then I would take him to Middlesbrough, to a 'blues'. These unlicensed haunts sell alcohol and are particularly popular with black people. Usually they are converted in a rough-and-ready way from terraced houses or sometimes disused commercial premises. Once the pubs and clubs had closed, people would want the party to go on and that is how blues parties developed. At one time, some cans of booze and a few grams of white powder or cannabis would get things going, but then they became more commercialised and people started to make money out of running blues parties where hundreds of people would pack in and an old boy would be on the door taking the entrance fee.

Some bullshit law had come out, the blacks said, that allowed them to open a blues because of their religion. The windows would be boarded up but the lights would be on and reggae-type music blasting out. Curry and rice would be served and plenty of drugs would be on sale to keep the party in full swing, while reggae tunes blasted out at full power. There would be plenty of prostitutes and illegal gambling would take place in the quieter rooms either upstairs or at the back of the house. Usually an open fire was kept going to quickly burn drugs if the police raided. They were very dangerous places, where you could get stabbed in the back. Lee Duffy was shot in a blues and he was killed outside another.

So I was jumping about in this blues with these lads Speedy and my mate Paddy, who were saying, 'Fucking hell, Brian knows everyone.'

I'm not showing off but I went to Redcar or this town or that town and everywhere I went, I would get in for nothing. At all the nightclubs and pubs the doormen would say, 'All right, Brian.'

I was taking too many Es and had stopped training. I'd let myself go, so I went back to training for about six months and took off about two stone. I was working in a club where these lads were selling gear and doing this and that, and a friend of David Garside [British and world boxing heavyweight title contender] got taxed in there. I had taken money off them in there as they were selling gear, so they came down to get the money back.

A rave had been going on for three days and everyone was full of ecstasy. Somebody was at the club with a phone, telling Garside my movements, and he made his way over there to fight me.

I'd been there since the Thursday, fucking E'ing, and had taken about 20-odd ecstasy as well as drinking Bacardi and Coke.

On the Sunday morning, about nine or ten o'clock, I was sitting with Newcastle's Robby Armstrong and he said, 'Fucking hell, big fella, you want to get home.' He was mopping my brow with a tissue because the sweat was pouring out of me. 'Go on, big fella, get yourself home,' he said, then left.

The raving madness was coming to an end and there were now only about 100 stragglers left in a club that had held a couple of thousand.

One doorman came and warned me, 'Garside is outside with two or three cars full of lads with hammers and bars and everything. Just fucking get out the back door.'

'I'm not running from no fucker,' I told him.

I went outside and Garside said, 'We want the fucking money that you took off the lad.'

10 GARSIDE VS COCKERILL I AND II

SETTING FOOT INTO daylight for the first time in three days, I felt like a battery hen! After coming out from a place that was in virtual darkness except for the strobe lighting, the daylight hurt my eyes like sand in a desert storm.

As I was trying to get my focus, Garside was standing there side on. He was a big fella. You could see he was a boxer because of his stance. Anyway, he had held the British heavyweight title and was ranked tenth in the world in one of the boxing magazines. He had been doing a lot of training and apparently was making a comeback to try and regain his heavyweight crown.

This looked like a tough one, as I was wrecked from three days of non-stop raving. One of us was going to wake up sore the next day! I headbutted him three times and he was out on his feet! I couldn't believe my luck. Here I was, half the man I knew I could be, and I had blitzed Garside. I never threw either a right or a left hook.

I bragged, 'I've beaten you, now. Look at you!'

I was showing off, being a dickhead. I would have destroyed him in a fight if I had been normal. He slumped back and blindly grabbed hold of me as if he was in the ring. We began to wrestle and after two or three minutes I got him up and threw him over my back and he crashed to the floor. I should have used this opportunity to stamp my authority all over his face, because that would have been the finish, and then I would have bitten his fucking nose off and pulled his eye out or something, but I didn't!

I pulled him against the wall and bit right through his ear and it was hanging on by the lobe. Later he got it stitched back on, but you can still see a memento of the occasion. We got in a bear hug and I was fucking knackered because of the rave. By now, the fight had been going on for about ten minutes. I was stuck in this floor position and I'd got him in a headlock when a lad said something to me. Fucking hell, I thought he had said, 'You've killed him,' but he had just said, 'You are killing him.'

I was strangling my opponent, so I let go of him, got up and braced my hand against a taxi. I was fucked! He came up behind me and hit me in the ribs with a body shot. It was the first time I had ever been sat on the floor like that.

This fight was getting the better of me and I was thinking, You can't beat me, I am unbeatable, I am the best. But I had a broken rib, so I couldn't breathe, and then he stuck a couple of boots in. About a hundred people, a lot of them big men, were watching the fight, and taxi drivers were standing on their taxis.

I wouldn't back down and I was trying to get up, but there was nothing left in me. I looked and Christine, my girlfriend at the time, said, 'Fucking hell, he's off his head, he's been on the gear all night.' She tried to help me but it was no good.

Garside, who had been in bed all night, was fresh as a daisy. On his side, Dave Woodier from Middlesbrough was the only one who jumped in and said, 'Come on, fucking hell, Dave.'

Woodier was kicking me and I was still trying to get back up, but then the fight was broken up and Garside was jumping about saying words to the effect that he was the Daddy. Then his lads took over the door.

Glover (David Jr) and all the other scumbags were saying they were going to do this and do that. Fucking arsehole, he is. His mates were going to kill me and shoot me and I said, 'Fuck 'em.'

I came away with a broken rib and a closed eye, but they were only superficial injuries. I was depressed because I had lost this fight and until then had never been beaten in my life. And I was fucking depressed because I had beaten myself through not training. I was so annoyed! I ran and reran the slo-mo action of the fight through my head for a million and one grilling times and, no matter how I played it, the result was always the same.

I went to see Little Frankie Atherton and I know it sounds daft, but it was like when the character from the *Rocky* films got beaten and he went to see Little Mickey. Well, that is what Frankie was like to me. Like Mickey, he is only little.

He told me, 'Get yourself right. Get off that fucking gear. I knew you shouldn't have been on it,' and gave me a fucking good bollocking.

I started training again with a vengeance, and started running. I had gone down to about 18 stone. I built myself up to 20 stone by training like fuck in Redcar. It was like going to a training camp and keeping out of the way of everyone.

People were offering to come with me when I had my second fight with Garside. A certain Middlesbrough firm said, 'We'll come down and help you.' I ended up getting some lads from Newcastle to come with me and we went to the club – I don't want to mention its name. It was a big, big firm from Newcastle and about 70 of them met me and we went down for my fight.

When we got to the club, there were police on the front and Garside had about 50 doormen from Liverpool and Manchester on the doors. Fuck it, we boltcutted the back door and went into the club, down the stairs, and he was somewhere inside.

I said, 'Where is Davey?'

'He's in the office,' the guy replied.

The office was about 12 foot square and there was a desk, a filing cabinet and something else. He was in there with another lad, a gangster from Liverpool, and I was with Paddy, not a great fighter but a very dangerous lad with weapons. Speedy was in jail.

We went in and Paddy said, 'Brian wants a fight for ten grand' and 'We will have a 20-grand fight,' and all that shit, but it was never fucking going to happen.

Garside told him, 'I wouldn't like to fight him in a second fight because the first fight I fucking struggled, and he was off his fucking head for three days on the drugs.'

He said he hadn't been training, 'So I don't really want a second fight.'

When this news came back to me, it made me even more determined.

I remember the night before I'd been up to Newcastle with Christine to see Stevie and Michael Sayers at Viv Graham's club. We had a few drinks. Afterwards Christine couldn't sleep because she knew I was seeing Garside the next day.

That night, at Viv Graham's club, Michael said, 'If he (Viv) comes up here just give him it. He'll be in tonight.'

I said, 'I'll fight anyone, I'm ready.'

What had happened a few months before is of relevance here. I was in this rave club and there was no real trouble. There were a few fights and I brayed a few bullies. Robby Armstrong came up to me and said, 'Do you know Brian Cockerill?'

I said, 'Yeah, I know him well.'

Robby asked, 'What's he like, can he fight?'

I replied, 'Yeah, he can fight a bit.'

He pushed me for more, 'What do you think he would do against Viv?'

I said, 'Well, I think he is bigger and stronger and I think he would beat him, personally.'

Then he said, 'Who the fuck is he?'

Then I said, 'Well, I'm Brian Cockerill!'

He went, 'Fucking hell!'

Because he only knew me as 'Big Bri', he never knew my second name.

It turned out that a lad called Smiggy had paid five grand for Viv to come down and have a fight with me. But Viv didn't come down, and that was why Robby was sussing things out now.

In the meantime, people were saying, 'You'll beat him, you're bigger. Lee told us you would beat him.'

So Robby said, 'Viv doesn't want a fight with you.'

'I don't know what you're on about,' I told him.

This was supposed to be a 50-grand fight between me and Viv that the big firm from Newcastle were supposed to be arranging. The next thing I knew, we were supposed to have this fight in a warehouse, because Lee Duffy was meant to have had his fight with Viv in a warehouse.

The firm said, 'We'll put £50,000 down on the table for Brian to fight Viv.'

Obviously, Viv Graham was a thorn in their sides and they wanted me to do the clearing up, as he was stopping them from going on his territory.

So when I was up in Newcastle, I went to Madison's nightclub, where Viv was supposed to be in every Friday night, and I got stopped at the door. I had an old tracksuit on and I said, 'Here, I came to see you with this flea-bitten, fucking tracksuit. Fuck suits.'

You are not allowed to go into Madison's wearing tracksuits or things like that, but what could they do? So I went in and was having a bit of a laugh with Stevie and Michael Sayers, Stevie Abadom and others. I think Viv had brayed Stevie Sayers and Stevie Abadom a couple of months before in that same club.

Stevie Sayers said, 'Will you have a fight with him for us?'

Viv never turned up, which was very strange, because for two years he was in there every Friday. I didn't know if they were just bulling me up. I think Friday was Viv's big night out.

That out of the way, the following night I went down to the rave club to fight Garside. I hadn't slept because I couldn't sleep thinking about it. This was a fight that meant a lot to me as it was all about restoring my confidence. It wasn't some barroom brawl. After our first fight, I thought, Fucking hell, I have been beaten for the first time! But then people were saying, 'Well, that wasn't you, that was some two or three stone lighter man.'

I could now understand where Lee Duffy was coming from when I beat him. For six weeks, I couldn't sleep properly. It felt fucking awful, like I was the king and then I wasn't the king.

It reminds me of when I had my fight with Dave Williams, the best fighter in Redcar. He was the one who had bullied me when I was 19 or 20. What happened now was that Williams was giving this lad some things to sell and the lad couldn't sell them because they weren't the proper merchandise. The lad got a good hiding from him; they beat up this lad, who was only about 11 stone. It was the main protagonist thinking he was the big hard man. He thought he was Godzilla. I would estimate he was about 16 stone and five foot eight – the muscular effect. He brayed this lad, so I fucking said, 'Right, I will fight him.'

So old China, who used to live in Redcar but has died now – may God rest him in peace. Is there anyone I know still alive? – said, 'Oh, Brian, come and do me a favour, come and have a fight with this cunt.'

Well, this cunt was the best fighter for over ten years. He was like Lee Duffy, the best fighter, so there are all these best fighters

I have fought and beaten. I have never ever been beaten by them. I went down to fight Dave Williams and there he was, on the seafront in Redcar, sitting in an Opal Manta.

I said, 'Get out of the fucking car, you shithouse.'

He said, 'No, you are too big.'

I repeated, 'Get out of the fucking car!'

The cunt wouldn't get out of the car, so I told my mate who was with me to stab him in the leg and he said, 'If you don't get out of this car and fight him, I'm going to fucking stab you in the head.'

With this in mind, Williams got out of the car. He took his top off and I thought he was going to start dancing about, but then he ran and grabbed me by the legs and tried to pick me up. This was when I was heavy and I fucking picked him up, nutted him, smashed him into the car, pulled him down and nutted him again at the bottom. I sat on top of him and poked my thumbs in his eyes, which began popping blood all over the place, so I had blood on me. This tosser was screaming and it was like something out of a Vincent Price film.

'Have you had enough, have you had enough?' I said.

I whacked him two more times in the face and in the body and people were shouting, 'Kill him, Brian. Kill the bastard!'

They hated him. And that was the end of that. They never saw him again. He retired after that but he was a bad bum, with a white beard. He was a horrible, heavy cunt who used to bully people. His dad was the same; he used to work in the gym and they used to say, 'I'll fight you for your wages.' They were just bullies, and the people they beat would end up with no wages that week.

To return to Garside, what I was charged with was this: they said I had gone to the club with 70 lads armed with shotguns and handguns, machetes and baseball bats, all these fucking weapons, and that we had gone round the back and used boltcutters to get in, and the fight with Garside is said to have taken place in this little room. Believe what you want, but I was supposed to have punched him with the right hand and this, allegedly, dropped him and he fell on the floor and was kicked about like an old cabbage.

Apparently, he went, 'Brian, Brian,' and put his hands over his face to try to stop me hitting him. He fell to the floor and I must have hit him 25 times in the face, kicked him to fuck, stamped all over his face, and he was shouting, 'Mercy, mercy, have mercy on me.'

A little cosh fell out of his pocket and I brayed the cunt with that as well. I said to him, 'Like you had mercy on me in the first fight.'

That fight had been a big mistake because I'd fucking let him get up and have a go at me and let him have a finish in the fight. But this time I fucking broke his jaw in six places, cheekbone, nose, head, and that was the end of him.

Garside said to Bam Bam, 'I believe your mate nearly killed me.' That's what he told him in Liverpool.

Bam Bam said to him, 'Dave, I believe that they had to put butter on your ears to get you through the ambulance doors, your head swelled that much with your brain in.'

The police came to the club and, when I say the police came, I mean the fucking police came; they came from Newcastle, Peterlee and all over!

They believed I had something to do with it because, when they went inside, one of the lads there said, 'Brian Cockerill's in there and they have got guns and everything and they have got machine guns.'

The police were already outside because the club had phoned them, and they had me down for the firearms, but then Newcastle Police were also involved because the heavy-duty Newcastle firm were supposed to have been there! And this Liverpool firm too, who were said to have had guns.

Well, I was supposed to have gone into the Eclipse and brayed Garside.

Anyway, he made a statement to the police saying that I had brought up 60 or 70 lads. But he never said the names, just that he was beaten up by certain lads in a club, big lads. Give him his due: he didn't name the big lads.

That night, the police were everywhere in that club, like at a football match: 20 there, 10 here, 50 over there. I would say there were about 200 of them. When they came for me, there were 20 of them all the way up the stairs of the club, like a guard of honour. Every step had a copper on and I walked through the middle of them and they parted like the Red Sea.

There were maybe 600 people in that club when I allegedly bashed Garside, and every person there must have come up to me to shake my hand, and every girl was kissing me on the cheek and grabbing me, because they were all happy because when I'd done the raves there was no bullying. They were taxing people, hitting people and they were just fucking bullies, so the typical crowd had gone down from 2,000 to 600. They finished it, killed the club, but, when I had it, it was brilliant.

So, when I came down the stairs there were 600 in there, and the police must have thought, Fucking hell, with all these people in here, if they kick off, we're in the shit. Half of the people were off their heads on drugs and it is hard to contain people when they're like that, because you can't talk to them. Anyway, they saw me and I presume they thought, Fuck it, let him go because there are too many people in.

When I walked out, there were about eight or nine inspectors in the cars, all with pips on their shoulders and all from separate police stations: Stockton, Thornaby, Middlesbrough and Newcastle. There were armed units all over, sitting about with guns, and there were fucking dog sections searching, but apparently the guns that we supposedly had were not found, so they never got me for that.

Everyone was happy because I had beaten a man who wasn't liked at the time, and I felt like king of the castle again. He knows that, when I go to bed and close my eyes, the last thing I see is me fucking braying him. He can tell people what he wants and they can say what they want.

I am not just on about this fight, but about every fight. You can't kid yourself. You have only got to close your eyes and you know what happens. I can go to sleep so happy. People say I had 60 or 70 lads with me. Well, I did, but that was because he had 50 fucking doormen and my lads were there just to make sure that it was a one-to-one fight. A straightener, as they call it in the business ... No hard feelings, Garside!

11 THE HAMMER HOUSE OF HORRORS

YOU WOULD THINK that would have been the end of it, but I got a phone call when I was at Tommy Harrison's house, in Teesside.

I thought I had seen somebody on a motorbike and I thought it was the police, because they were always pulling me up. I'd gone to see Tommy to tell him that I had beaten Garside. (I told Little Frankie Atherton the news too.) Later that day, when I was back at home, Tommy phoned and said, 'I have got some work for you, pop yourself over,' so I went over again.

Naturally, I thought that it was a follow-on from my news about the fight. When I got there, Chino and Steve Bradley were outside. Naturally, I thought that it was a follow-on from my news about the fight. When I got there, Chino and Steve Bradley were outside, they had nothing to do with what follows.

A lad with a bad eye answered Tommy's door and I entered the house like a lamb to the slaughter. The second I went in, 10 or 12 lads attacked me all at once, hitting me with fucking bars.

At the time, I was unaware of how I'd got into this trap of retribution. Tommy Harrison, Middlesbrough's elder statesman of the underworld, had been put in a very delicate situation when he faced the twin barrels of a shotgun. As he pushed the gun away from him, Tommy gave the person poking it into his face a few choice words of friendly advice.

What these people wanted was for Tommy to phone me and ask me to call around on some sort of pretext. At that moment, Tommy wasn't in a position to refuse this request. Some of my sources tell me that in no way did he ever suspect such violence would be used against me and that, if he had known what was going to happen, he would not have phoned me.

So, when I turned up there was a posse of armed men with handguns, a shotgun and all sorts of equipment used to butcher animals. I was then about 20 stone and, although I hadn't trained for some time, I was still very powerful, but I couldn't do anything against a 12-bore shotgun.

A fight took place that lasted for some time and left my legs badly hacked and my head smashed to an unsightly mess. Afterwards, Tommy's house resembled a house of horrors and, since some of the gory implements used on me were hammers, I think I can safely call it 'the hammer house of horrors'!

During the sustained butchering, a man came in, a man familiar to me, who tried, unsuccessfully, to break my jaw. Not a single bone in my body was broken, but my head and legs were a mishmash of gore. Really, I should have been dead, and a lesser man than me may well have been ended up in the morgue. Some time later, one of the attackers paid compensation to Tommy Harrison to cover the clean-up bill for his home.

A number of people were arrested and remanded in custody over this incident, but I didn't make any statement to the police and, as a consequence, no one was ever charged with this brutal and savage revenge attack on me, carried out by some of the more familiar underworld characters from Tyneside, Sunderland and Teesside.

A story from a dead underworld character, a friend of Speedy, indicates that, when Speedy was locked up serving time with one of the main players (who was serving time for a separate offence) in the attack against me, he was able to fully explain a side of the story that had been withheld and this changed his opinion of me and made him wish he had never been involved in the assault on me.

There were people there that I know, but I don't want to mention their names and I wouldn't do so. Steve Richards fully investigated this attack against me and he has an audiotape of interviews with independent sources naming those who attacked me. I am aware that this could result in criminal prosecutions against those who practically hacked my legs off, but, so long as those involved do not challenge this account, I am prepared to let things go.

When I went in, they all started hitting me with bars and hammers and someone pulled a gun on me and I knocked the gun out of his hands and pushed one of them over. I was fighting in the doorway, throwing them about. This was a big fucking firm from Newcastle – not the Sayers family.

I wouldn't say they were all great fighters, but they were dangerous people who have shot people, people who have been up for murders, people who have been up for killings and for torturing, people who have been up for drugs, anything dangerous. All violent people, they would make the Krays look like Mother Teresa and Ghandi, and I was doing fucking well against them.

I was fucking throwing them about like rag dolls while shitty arse, the man himself, was in the kitchen. He was asked by Steve Richards if he had been sitting next to a customs officer on a plane bound for Spain. He did all he could to deny it and

115

allowed the rest of what was written about him in this book to remain. This man was saying to the other 11 or so cabbaged souls to break my jaw. 'Break his jaw!'

He was trying to hit me in the face with a cosh and smashed it, but he didn't break anything. They hit me in the legs with baseball bats. Have you seen the film *Casino*, where you see one of the characters getting beaten in the face with a baseball bat? Well, that is something what it was like: they were fucking braying me and hitting me on the head. It was split open all over, blood from the holes in it was hitting the ceiling and I was trying to get back up to pull them down, but they were kicking me and fucking hitting me with bars. I think a lot of them were scared of me. They were doing well and I went down at the end, after an attack that went on for a long time: maybe six minutes.

After hitting me and stabbing me, they all started running off and I said, 'You, you cunt!'

The next fucking minute, Tommy Harrison was there and his son, Lee, and they ran to the house next door. Tommy's other son, Andrew, helped me into a car that was driven by Tommy's driver, Buster Atkinson, and he sped off taking me to the hospital. He took a blanket in the car and it was covered in blood. I couldn't walk because one of my legs was smashed to bits. I was trying to get to my car to drive myself there and I ended up lying on the bank with the teatime traffic going by.

At the hospital, the lad first took me to the maternity ward! After that little mistake was sorted out, I was attended to and had fucking stitches all over my body, my legs and my back where I had been stabbed. They stitched me up like an old three-piece suite. They ran out of anaesthetic and in the end they were stitching me without anaesthetic because I didn't feel it now.

As they were bashing me, the attackers were saying that my legs and arms had to be broken. But, although they beat me so much with baseball bats, there wasn't one broken bone. The

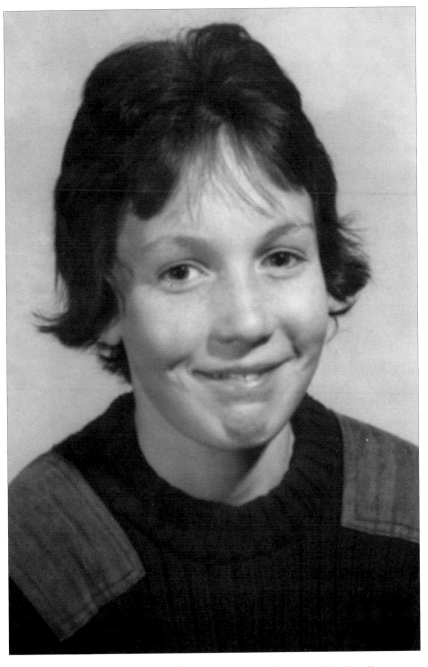

The Taxman as a young man. Me as a grinning 13-year-old schoolboy –
a bright future ahead.

Top: Football is a true passion. Here I am at 15 holding the school championship winner's cup. I was centre forward and had been made captain of the year.

Bottom left: Dressing up as kids at the Grey Thorp Club. This was for a fancy dress competition. I'm in the mummy outfit, and my brother Bobby won with the caveman suit. Peter in the Batman costume won the infants.

Bottom right: Christmas dinner with the family. A younger me sitting up to the table on the far right.

Pure muscle! These pictures show me in the Mr and Miss England
Competition 1986. I came 4th out of 21 finalists in the under 21s.
I'm fourth from the left in the line up.

Striking poses to show off those hard-won muscles...

Top: Silks nightclub, where I fought the police and kicked the doors off a van!

Bottom: The place where I fought the infamous Lee Duffy in Redcar.

Top left: My pride and joy, my motorbike.

Top right: My wife, Amanda, the love of my life.

Bottom: Me and the family. From left to right is my sister, Christine, my father, James, a sneaky looking Steve Richards (who helped me write this book) holding Harley the Wonder Dog, myself and my youngest brother, Jamie.

Top: With the Cockerill name on your door, the wrong sorts won't come knocking.

Bottom: Me on top form with friend Andrew Hutt. Successful actor Andrew is the Duffer lookalike who was set to play Lee Duffy in a film on his life.

Happy days. With my son Jordan (*top*) living it up in the Dominican Republic, and relaxing in the pool.

doctors were amazed. I was bruised all colours of the rainbow: purple, yellow, black, blue and the rest.

The police were straight on to it because when you go to hospital in cases like this the hospital has to inform them. Besides, when my assailants left the house, people had seen the cowards running away with their machetes and handguns, and blood all over them, and I had been seen coming out of the house in a state.

When I was in hospital, the police were there and I was put under armed arrest, not just for this incident but also because I'd beaten up Garside the week before. So there I was in hospital and the police were sitting there too; it was like something out of *The Sweeney* or *Minder* from years ago. Every six hours they changed shift, 24 hours a day.

Stevie and Michael Sayers came to see me. There were villains from all over the fucking place wanting to help me. I was getting two or three hours a day for visits and I was getting between 50 and 70 visitors a day, every single day. Everyone was allowed about two minutes to see me and then it would be, 'Right, time is up.' At times, there was a queue of 40 or 50. People must have liked me because when I bashed them I wasn't a bully. You might class me as a bully with the drug dealers, but that's a different thing. When I'm in the pub and someone nudges into me, I say, 'All right, mate, how you doing?'

The police asked, 'Will you make a statement?'

I said, 'No!'

They cajoled, 'Look, you're going to have to make a statement!'

'Look, I'm making no statement!' I told them.

When the police asked me how I ended up in such a state I said, 'I fell down some steps, you know what I mean.'

I'm the old school, like the staunch character in the old Jimmy Cagney-type films. If you dish it out, you have to be able to take it. If I was dying on the floor, with two seconds to live and they said, 'Who killed you?' I still wouldn't tell them, because what purpose would it serve? Somebody going to jail is not the answer. And, of course, the community would brand me a crybaby and shun me. Don't get me wrong: I want to get them back and fucking bray them or put them in a hole somewhere or shoot the cunts. If I wanted to get them back, I would get someone to go and shoot the bastards or take them away somewhere. That would be classed as getting them back.

I gained strength while in hospital from knowing I'd beaten Garside the week before. When I recovered, I saw him. I went into the pub and chided him, 'Do you want another fucking one?'

He baulked at the idea and said, 'No, I've had two of yours. I don't want any more.' He was just fucking terrified.

I saw him few months ago and shouted out of the car window, 'Now then, you piehead, I don't know how you made any money from boxing with a head that big.'

He dropped his head and went on. His strength was jumping about in the street. When I battered him, I am supposed to have broken his granite jaw in six places, absolutely shattered his jaw, I didn't just break it, I shattered it all over, and so I was over the fucking moon.

When he beat me, all I got was a black eye. By comparison, what I got in that house was way beyond what he got from me. This is what gave me strength as I lay simmering in the hospital; this is what got me through the anguish and the pain in the hospital after nearly being killed. That is the only way anyone could beat me. People couldn't do it one-to-one, but, the first fight I lost, I beat myself really and it won't happen again. But it is good to get beaten in a way, because then you feel the bitter taste of losing.

The people who were in the house of horrors had been grassed up by David Glover (junior) because he was a police informant. That was him, the fucking rodent. He made some statement in which he said, 'We didn't go to Stockton to beat him up; we came down to kill Brian Cockerill.'

I was shown the statement by Phil Berriman when I was visiting his home. Glover could have just been exaggerating when he was on about them planning to kill me, in order to get off with his own serious charges, so I take what his statement said with a pinch of salt.

Whether they wanted to kill me or just beat me up, I kept fighting back and I wouldn't give in. There were a lot of people in that house and I think they came down to get me and put me down. Maybe they were going to try to shoot and kill me by using Glover, masked up on a motorbike while I was in the car driving. That is what I presumed they meant when they said they were coming to kill me.

They wouldn't have tried to kill me in the house because there were too many witnesses. When they were hitting me on the head, someone said, 'No! Not on the head, no more!'

They were smashing away at my head with full-sized baseball bats, splitting it open like an old beanbag. I have still got indentations from it. There were more than four witnesses there, young lads who were watching the mob set about me.

The police wanted to move me to another hospital. In order to fool anyone hanging around waiting to kill me, they had two ambulances: one was for me and the other one was a decoy.

There were police marksmen on the roofs and armed police running with me. It was like something in the movies: as they rushed me from my wheelchair into the ambulance, these coppers were belting out orders to each other like, 'Go now!' They would be peering around corners from beneath their SWAT-style caps to ensure I didn't get shot.

I was in hospital for ten days and the staff were understandably nervous with all the guns about and didn't want me in the place. In those ten days, I had two operations to save my legs. The wounds were so bad they had to cut the already gored limbs open even more to relieve the pressure. This woman doctor – she was beautiful – came in and she saw me and I thought, She can't be a doctor, she's only about 25.

The bombshell news delivered by this drop-dead-gorgeous doctor was more frightening than anything I had ever heard in my life: 'You are going to lose your leg.'

Lose a leg, fucking hell! I was feeling rather fragile. Even my fingers were shivering at the thought of losing a leg. I would be an amputee! I could hear them now: 'Come on, son, let the cripple through', 'Mind out of the way for the one-legged bastard' and 'Ah, so you're the entrant in the one-legged arse-kicking competition.'

When that mob had brayed it, they had damaged all the nerves and the blood was seeping out of the veins, so it was getting bigger and bigger. In a gamble to save my leg, the surgeons opened it up and fiddled about inside. They had to take some skin off the top of it to graft on the lower leg and then bandage the whole pile of tripe up. Sounds simple, but it was a little more complicated than that! I was purple and black all over. I looked like the Ribena man, fucking ridiculous, and my head had ballooned up to the size of a big beach ball, it was that bad, and my ears were all purple. I looked like I should have been dead.

My size had saved my life. The doctor told me that a lesser man would have died and it was my muscle tissue that had saved me. The bars and baseball bats had hit the muscle, not the bone.

But the thing that got me through it was that I had beaten Garside the week before. I had beaten him one-to-one, just him and me; no fucker else beat him. That was my yes factor and that was good.

I said, 'I can't see all the lads going to jail,' so I went and I got them all off. I said that they were my mates. Would you believe that, after all the hospital business, all the fucking trauma, all that and me nearly fucking dying and losing two pints of blood, I was arrested!

The doctors really wanted to keep me there, but, because of the police, they wanted to get rid of me. If the police hadn't been at the hospital, I probably would have been there three or four weeks. I was in and out in ten days. You could tell all the doctors and staff were on edge. So they moved me out and said, 'Go home and we'll have the district nurse come round every day.'

My dressings needed changing daily. You could see the muscle and bones in my leg when you took the bandages off. The hole was deep, about two inches wide and ran all the way from my knee to my ankle.

Anyway, when I came out, the head copper said, 'Can I have a word with you, Brian? You will only be half-an-hour or so.'

They took me off in a wheelchair and they fucking arrested me! I was in a wheelchair and had these crutches and they arrested me and kept me in the cells for two fucking days. I ended up getting an infection in my leg and this fucking poxy police doctor came and gave me two paracetamols, the wanker. When I was in hospital, I was on morphine tablets for the pain. The fucking bastards. I wouldn't show the police the pain I was in. I was in dire fucking agony and I couldn't have a piss because the toilets cubicles in those cells are fucking tiny and you are struggling to fit in.

Eventually I went to court. I couldn't get up the stairs from the cells and the sweat was coming out of me like bullets. It would have been easier to dance on the head of pin than to climb those stairs in the state I was in. You would have thought I had just been training or something. The pain was like nothing I had experienced on earth. The screws there were disgusted and said, 'This is ridiculous, taking a man to court like this!'

I had to take all this medication, which was given to me from my police property bag when I was taken from the cells to the court. The solicitor had a list as long as my arm detailing the treatment I needed: three types of painkillers, a nurse coming round every day, cream on this and things on that. Well, you can't get all that in jail. I was given bail but I couldn't walk anyway. The bail conditions were that I couldn't go into any pubs in Teesside.

I went home with Christine and stayed there and she looked after me all the time and kept me right. In the end, there was nothing to prove I had attacked Garside, so the case against me was thrown out of court.

I was only 26 and I had beaten every fighter in the North-East that I had ever come up against. When I was 23, 24, I had beaten everyone in Teesside.

To end this chapter, I'll tell you about an interesting event that happened a few weeks after I came out of hospital. I was now more vigilant than ever and followed people's every movement just in case anyone was going to finish the job the mob had half done.

A friend had driven me back home and, as we headed into my estate, I noticed a dark car being driven slowly. The first thing I spotted about the dark-skinned driver was that he was wearing a pull-down woolly hat on his head. The man fitted the bill for a hitman: a dark car and a hat to pull down over his face when he shot me.

I said to my friend, 'Pull over here, let's see where this guy is going.'

By this time we were a few doors away from my home and the dark car was heading towards the cul-de-sac at the end of my street; it would have to stop soon. It did, but the driver turned it round and was heading back in our direction, very slowly.

I could see him craning his neck to take a look at the door

numbers, and as he headed towards us his headlights dazzled us, so we were like sitting ducks, and my legs weren't in any condition to run!

I worked out that, by the time we had reversed away, he would be upon us and shooting, so I was better off out in the open rather than staying put in the car.

'Fucking hell,' I said to my friend, 'we'd better get out before he gets any closer.'

The car was about 30 yards away and still trundling along at walking pace, with the driver still craning his neck and looking frantically from left to right. I had to get out of the car and draw him away from my home. There was no time for heroics; this was a pro and he meant business! I flung the door open, threw my crutches out by the side of the car, then reached out and gripped the roof gutter and heaved my colossal frame out of the car. The car tilted to the side as I clung to the roof. Tentatively, I put my weight on my legs as quickly as I could manage and for a moment, I danced about like a drunken spider.

Lights flashed before my eyes as pain took hold. Beads of sweat were forming on my forehead as the adrenalin surged through my veins. I stumbled to the back of the car to look like I was getting something from the boot. I thought maybe the hitman would see me and recognise me and, if so, he might think I was opening the boot to get a weapon out.

The car came to a hesitant stop right outside my front door and the swarthy driver exited from it sharpish. I noticed he had a brown paper bag in which he would have concealed his gun, probably a sawn-off shotgun. Aiming a handgun with precision would have taken more time, but a shotgun is a simple point-and-shoot tool and has a wide spread of shot. The bag would prevent the spread of cordite from the gun, thus reducing any chances of the gunman failing a police forensic test, if caught.

Time stood still for me as this brutal-looking character made his way up my garden path. Fuck the pain, I thought.

I shouted to my friend to drive his car at the hitman, 'Drive at him! Fuck the bushes!'

My friend fired up the engine, revved the engine and the car jolted forward. He had fucking stalled it! By this time, I had made my move. Bad legs or not, I was within feet of the cunt. Already he had rung my doorbell and Christine would be answering it. Just another couple of steps and I would be in killing distance. My legs were fucked, but I could still snap him in half with my raw upper-body strength!

Just at that moment, the door to my house opened and the man said, 'Takeway delivery.'

I was within a hair's breadth of severely hurting this man and it was only a fucking takeaway deliveryman! How could I be so sure? Because the bag was partly crushed and the sauce from one of the aluminium containers had leaked its oily contents through the bag. And for confirmation, Christine said, 'Yes, thanks,' and then looked at me and said, 'I thought I'd get us a nice lamb rogan josh for supper.'

I waved frantically at my friend, who was having difficulty trying to start his car, and shouted, 'It's all right, it was just a takeaway driver.'

Christine gave me a quizzical look, as I did not have my crutches.

'Oh, I was just seeing if I could manage a few steps without my crutches,' I gasped as I leaned against the porch, drenched in sweat.

12 INSTANT JUSTICE

I WAS ONLY in the house a fortnight while my legs were slowly mending, but boredom soon set in. No longer in the shadow of Lee Duffy, I went out and taxed these lads who were selling Es. I went in and took £1,000 off them while still on my crutches!

The coppers were stopping me all the time, pulling me on motorways, and drug dealers were paying me money to stop me taxing them. I was going to dealers' houses and getting 100 quid off them, and then every fucker that was a dealer was saying they were working for me because other people were trying to tax them but wouldn't dare tax Brian Cockerill's lads.

People in pubs would say, 'That coke you are selling is nice, Brian.'

I would say, 'What coke? I'm not selling coke.'

'That lad over there is selling it for you,' they used to say.

I would go up to the unsuspecting dealer and demand, 'Give me the money, then, if it's mine!'

Young lads were running about telling everyone that they

were selling it for me! I was on the door in Stockton when there was this fight and I threw the troublemaker out.

He blasted, 'You think you're hard, don't you? Wait until my brother comes.'

'Oh, yeah. Who is your brother?' I enquired.

'Brian Cockerill,' he said.

Laughing, I replied, 'Well, go and fucking get him then.'

I have heard that line a few times.

We were running about taxing this one and taxing that one and an opportunity would come up when someone would say, 'He's got ten kilos.'

You would infiltrate a gang of, say, three lads, Tom, Dick and Harry. You would go and see Tom and say, 'Look, Tom, I'll be coming in when you're doing the deal with Dick and Harry. You're all going to have 60 grand's worth of gear for nothing. I'll come round menacingly and take the gear and the money off you all when you do the deal, and make it look as if I'm taking their money off them and taking your gear off you. I'll be coming in with a sports bag and will be taking a sports bag from you, but that bag will be stuffed with old newspapers to look like it's got your gear in it. Then I take their £60,000 and walk out of the door.'

Of course, Tom would be over the moon because after feigning rage at being taxed he would still have his gear. Dick and Harry would have lost their money and wouldn't be buying any drugs for a while, so it was a way of keeping the drug money off the streets. And then, of course, it didn't mean to say I wouldn't be calling back on Tom to relieve him of his drug stash and send it to the heavens in a billow of flames.

I have done other taxes where I have taken ten grand from two of them and have put fuck all in, as it was just paper in the bag. I have taken 20 grand and there wouldn't be any comebacks.

I remember another one, Garside's mate, the one who brought

him to the first fucking fight. The lad who was with him was selling blow, cannabis resin, and he wanted ten kilos off this lad called Les, in Winny Banks. A lad called Flea was with me and another couple, Steve and Robbie.

I said, 'We'll have this cunt over!'

It was worth over £10,400 for ten kilos because it was £400 for the lad's wages for running about. I will show you how we did it. You would get what is called a nine bar of blow – that's nine ounces.

The buyer would say, 'Look, before we do the deal, can I test it?'

I would say, 'Yes, the lad has got it in the bag.'

You would put your hand into the bag and rummage about as if there was loads in there and say, 'Here, will that do you?'

The gullible bastard would say, 'That's excellent, that,' and hand you £10,400.

The bag would be handed over and there would be fuck all in it but the one nine bar and some building bricks to make the weight up.

We would drive off after taking ten-and-a-half grand off him and it had cost us just 30p for the Lion bar, which looks like blow. So the four of us had made two-and-a-half grand apiece.

Sometimes you would make nine grand. You might get three ounces, mix it into nine and they think they are getting nine ounces. You give them a little bit of the end bits because these are pure gear. You take one of the corners off, test it and do what they do. Really, it is only three ounces, but the corners are pure.

They have got to roll a bit off, but you have got to remember the police are about. There might just be a quarter there, so you might have an ounce of coke but all the rest is fucking shit.

It is just like the fag deals. The other year the rumour on the street was that I was supposed to have taken £60,000 off three of them. The greedy cunts were selling cigarettes and making a fortune. They were bragging that they were making 100 grand here and 100 grand there and doing this and doing that. I wasn't powerful enough to take it off them, but then I got into one of their cliques and they told me when they were doing the money.

I told them, 'I want the money off the three of you.' Just like that.

Without any arguing, they gave me the 60 grand. The lad would tell me how much money they were turning over and they were turning over 100 grand a week! They gave me 60 grand to keep me away from them for two years. Well, it wasn't like taking it off them; it was like protection money.

After that, whatever they were doing, I wasn't bothered. They would go somewhere and buy cigarettes and then smuggle them through and sell them. I was simply their hired security. If you get caught with drugs, nine ounces of coke, say, you would get maybe fucking ten years behind bars. Compare that with being caught with 100 grand's worth of fags. You would get maybe two or three months for that, so they were doing cigarettes because there is no jail in it and lots of money.

Personally, I would say the drug game is finished because there are too many dealers and too many grasses in it now and it is just not the same as it used to be. The money is finished. Even the IRA are into their fags now. You can get massive amounts of money out of cigarettes. People are still making a lot of money out of cigarettes and they have got bent customs helping them make it. Of course, it depends on how big you are. The Lithuanians and the Russians make fortunes out of it.

One of the cigarette scams involves using blocks of wood. We would have blocks of wood, two inches by four inches, the same size as a carton of fags. You get somebody to make the carton wrappers and print them. You put the fake cartons in a bag and you might have 20,000 real fags in one particular bag, so as to calm any fears that you did not have the full quota you said you had. The buyer would obviously want to check the fags were real, and want to test them. This is where the real fags come into the equation. You could do this time and time again!

One of my gypsy pals spent about two grand on fags and made 20 grand with the block-of-wood scam. They would do the same with tins of cheap foodstuffs. They would buy a bulk load of something at a cost of a few pence per tin, have fancy labels made up and then sell the newly packaged items to unsuspecting shopkeepers. The shopkeeper's customers would complain that they had some grapefruit segments instead of some fancy product they thought they had bought!

One time we were running about all day and I knocked on this lad's door – he was the scumbag of Hartlepool – and he was standing there in a leopard-print leotard, like Tarzan or a circus strongman wears. His lass was in this rubber bondage gear. They were busy making a porno.

I said, 'I'm fucking cheetah, where's your drugs?'

They gave me so much money to leave them alone, funny bastards.

Then there was a Pakistani kid who was supposed to be getting heroin from a firm in Newcastle. He was running about all over selling it and he said, 'I'll give you a wage.'

He was supposed to give me a grand for every time he sold one. I don't condone using heroin. It is horrible stuff, it pickles people's souls. It is not just a matter of getting hooked, it is old people getting robbed. Horrible, horrible stuff. I just don't associate with it.

This kid was running about selling the stuff and what annoyed me was that people were saying, 'That brown you have got is good.' Just like the coke dealer who was saying it was my gear, this git was doing the same with the brown.

I was saying, 'I don't sell fucking brown or any drugs.'

Then somebody else would tell me the same, and somebody else.

Stevie Lancaster said, 'Everyone is saying you are selling brown!'

Then I got another phone call about it, so I was fucking fuming! I found out that it was the Pakistani kid.

I went to his house and I said, 'I want the fucking money!'

They were using my name for protection so they could peddle this filth on the streets. They gave me £21,000. Well, they gave me 14 grand and said the other seven grand was in the safe. 'We'll give you that later.'

We got the other seven grand and it was supposed to be from a big firm up in Newcastle who were into shooting people and the like.

Eventually a guy phoned me and said, 'There's a problem!'

I said, 'No! There's not a problem here. What's your problem?'

He said, 'Well, you have got our money, that is our money from our gear. You've taken our money.'

I shouted down the phone, 'So fuck, you shouldn't be running about in Teesside thinking you are a big hard man, your firm and that.'

The same man was recently nicked in Tenerife for 10,000 Es. He got chased out of Newcastle after someone bit off the end of his nose because he was playing at being the hard man.

This very scumbag of a man phoned me up and I said, 'Listen here, you mug, you don't give a fuck who you have got and blah, blah, blah.'

He threatened, 'Well, I'm coming down with the lads to sort you out.'

I snarled, 'Well, fucking come down then.'

So I got about 200 lads together. We didn't need that many but I thought, I will show this cunt. I went to the gypsy caravans and got the gypsy kids together, then I went to see a load of other firms and got them involved. You want a fucking war, I'll give you a fucking war, I thought.

He is an arsehole; he never came down when he said he would. He came down about two weeks later, kidnapped the Pakistani lad and went to see Louis Walsh to have me sorted out. For those of you not in the know, Louis Walsh is a big name in the gypsy community and the unlicensed boxing fraternity. He fights for big purses of prize money and he's a top fighter, the best in Darlington.

They asked Louis, 'Will you have a fight with this lad for 11 grand?'

He said, 'I'll fight any fucker for 11 grand. Who is the lad I am fighting?'

They said, 'Brian Cockerill.'

He exclaimed, 'You daft cunt, Brian Cockerill!' as if the guy was joking.

Then Louis asked who the fight was for and when he found out he said, 'Well, he's a fucking grass anyway,' and slapped him.

Because he was my pal, Louis told me, 'They're trying to get you fucking done here,' and he said, 'Well, I'm on your side.'

They were fucked because my firm was too big for their firm, and that was because everyone likes me. Even when I have a fight with someone, I don't carry it on. Once I have had a fight with someone, it is finished with, we don't carry it on, we don't keep going on and on, we don't keep going back and hitting someone. To do that would be like bullying them, and I know from my school days what it is like to be bullied.

That is why Lee Duffy died, through going back time after time and beating David Allison, known as Allo. Lee had beaten him two or three times and that is why it all ended in Lee's untimely death. Allo was scared. He could do one of three things: he could run away, come out fighting or go to the police.

He didn't run away, because he wasn't a run-away type, and he wouldn't go to the police because he is not the type to go to the police. He was pushed into a corner.

I remember the night when Mark Hartley, who was with Lee when he was stabbed, told me that he was trying to keep him alive and was saying, 'Keep your eyes awake, Lee, keep awake.'

I had nightmares after that. Mark is a nice lad; he just sells pigeons and things like that.

That night, Lee told Mark, 'See him, he is the best fighter that I have ever seen in my life.' He was talking about me.

There was another mate of mine who could fight, Kevin Allen. He was only a little lad, but he could fight. He was a lovely lad, but he's dead now.

Another black firm came and they had a lad called who was working with a lad down here. He was a big, big drug dealer from Leeds. I can mention his name now because he was shot dead. He came down here, running about selling heroin, and I was annoyed.

There was going to be a little bit of a war. I was in Spain or Greece on holiday and I got a phone call from my mate saying this black firm had supplied some brown to one of the Teesside lads. The lad had given it to someone I knew and this person had lost it. The lad blamed my mate for losing it. He also named another lad.

The black firm came down to shoot them, two or three carloads of black men with an Uzi or two, and they kidnapped one lad and they brayed him and held him for three days with a gun pointed at him.

Anyway, I phoned them and said, 'You want a fucking war, you come down here.'

Once again, I had to round up the troops. I got all the lads together waiting for them, but then they turned back and fucking went back to Leeds.

They phoned me and I said, 'The lads are going to pay you the money for what they lost. You will have the money by Monday.'

Come the Monday, the lads let me down and fucked off. They made me look like a mug.

The black lad phoned me again and said, 'You've got some bottle, you. Maybe it should be you we are working for.'

I said, 'I'm not into selling drugs, mate. I'm not into selling shit like that, no disrespect to you, but I just do taxing and things like that. I am a tax man, I am not into drugs.'

So he was all right with me. Someone said he left about three million in his will to his mum, he was so successful. He had been shot about four or five times over the years, but that is not the way to live. And he was in Ingleby Barwick, south of Stockton, where a police operation nicked him. I can say all this now because these people are dead and these other two lads were wanted in New York for six shootings. They had killed six people and they were taken back to the States and either given the death penalty or a prison term.

The police must have heard conversations when we were talking to this black lad and put two and two together and come up with fucking ten again, thinking that I had been doing gear with this bloke. But I wasn't: I was sorting fucking trouble out for people.

In the meantime, I was running about Middlesbrough doing a few things. At the time, the police had set up surveillance against me and used a gym owner called Micky Flanagan.

Flanagan owned a gym in Yarm, near my home, where I trained, but clearly he was also working with the police. I noticed he was getting skinnier every week. Now, I am very good at psychology, picking up on people's thoughts. He's setting me up, I thought to myself.

He was saying, 'The police have had me in.'

He had lost his kids to his girlfriend, who had won custody of them, and she was living with a mate of mine, a black lad called Rudy.

Then Rudy got turned round and said to me, 'He is trying to set us up for something I haven't even done.'

I went out with Micky Flanagan, I was looking after his kids at the weekend and I was helping to pick them up for him and doing all sorts for the scumbag – and he was working with the police. He was working with this copper who had been on Operation Ronson at a time when all the other coppers were said to have been on cocaine and were put in rehab.

The coppers would bust a house and get three ounces of coke, recut it with whatever they put in it, glucose or something like that, and the defendant would still be done for three ounces, but it would be weaker, and the police would keep one and a half ounces for themselves.

Girls I know have become secretaries for the police and they told me that at the weekend officers would say, 'Are you going out, girls? Do you want a couple of grams?'

They do the same with cannabis. They can't cut that, but they raid a small house and just confiscate it. They are just as much tax men as I am. Yes, they are tax men, just the same as me, but they are legal tax men, the bastards.

I remember when this boy's motorbike was stolen. I got a phone call from his dad, 'My son's bike has been stolen, can you help get it back?'

He had saved about £600 for this bike and people were telling him that I was the only person who might be able to help him now.

I knew where the bike was, so I went and sorted it out and told him, 'Go and pick it up.' I finished off by saying, 'Whatever you can do, stop at the police station and give them your views;

they have been on the case for a fucking fortnight. Tell them Brian has got your son's bike back within three hours.'

13 THE NUMBER ONE
TAX MAN

THIS LAD AND his mates came to the Eclipse rave club and tried to take over the door for the weekend. I didn't run the door, others did that, but I used to get paid a wage to stop any trouble. All the Stockton firm and all the Middlesbrough firm wanted this lad done. There must have been about 500 kids in the club that night wanting to kill him.

Speedy wanted to shoot the troublemakers, so they fucked off and didn't take the door in the end. Nobody really bothered us. There was only Garside and, after that carry-on with him, the club got shut down.

After taxing a dealer for a grand, I was running about and I was in this blues and a girlfriend of Stuart Watson was there. Stuey is from Gateshead; he used to be on the rave scene and ran a few doors up in Newcastle, but then he got nicked and was charged with running a brothel empire!

This girl was saying, 'I'll get Stuey.'

I said to her, 'Shut up, you daft cunt.' I only said this because

I knew Stuey. 'Fuck off, you daft cunt,' I said. I pushed her gently aside and repeated, 'Fuck off!'

Then she left the blues but came back later. She didn't fucking come over and point at me, but she pointed me out to someone and then these two black lads came in. I knew they were either going for a handgun or a knife. I just saw the blade come out and I jumped and fucking sparked the guy with a left hook, dropped him and he crashed to the floor, and Smiler from Redcar kicked him in the head. He bashed the other one up and then they shut the blues down.

Another time I was in there with Speedy and this Asian kid called Ram was going to shoot him outside with a shotgun, so I went out and there were about 100 people there.

I said, 'If you are going to shoot anybody, shoot me, you daft cunt. With all these people here, you are going to shoot me? You are going to get yourself 25 fucking years. I'm going to be dead and I am not even going to think about it, so shoot me.'

He put the gun down and fucked off. I saw this lad again – he is 30-odd – only about three months ago when I was in the Jeep in Grove Hill where he lives now. He said, 'Can you remember when I pulled the gun on you, Brian, and I shit myself? I didn't dare shoot you.'

There have been some speedy fuckers going into these blues, some very dangerous people. I am not saying they could fight, because some couldn't even fight off sleep. But they are dangerous people, they haven't got brains and they would just trash you!

I was at a mate's house. I call him Dicky Dido and he is a boxer, a gypsy boxer. At the time I wasn't allowed to drink because I was on medication after the 'house of horrors' incident, and anyway I was barred from Middlesbrough pubs while on bail, so I went to pubs down Whitby way, in a little village where they are all into gypsies.

THE NUMBER ONE TAX MAN

We visited these little pubs, having a laugh – well, as much as I could while drinking non-alcoholic drinks. 'Come on, we'll go to the blues,' someone said. There were about six of us and we needed a couple of taxis to get there.

As there were no seats in the blues and I was on crutches, I wedged myself in the corner, leaning against the wall. I was with Smiler and Dicky's brother-in-law.

This lass of about 25 started some funny business with Dicky. I said, 'Just ignore her, she's daft.'

She shouted, 'You don't fucking bother me. If he stands watching me, I'll smash his fucking face in.'

These sorts of incidents involving women were rare for me. I just put it down to PMT.

We went back to Dicky's at Stokesley, south of Middlesbrough. They are all gypsies there and all their fights are one-to-one. I was there with Lee once and I had been drinking all day and doing sit-ups and one-arm press-ups. Lee used to be able to stand with his foot out and, with one leg, go all the way down and all the way back up. Although he was about 17 stone, he did this one-legged routine with ease.

That day I had 1,100 quid on me and earlier I'd taken £300 out of it to spend and kept the rest to take home for Christine. This £1,100 I'd taxed off some lads who had gone to Christine's house fucking full of ecstasy, acid and drink. She had told them I was out.

When I found out about it, I fumed, 'I'm going to fucking kill them when I get my hands on them!'

What annoyed me more than anything was that when I went after them they were shitting themselves, even though they had all been running about with shotguns and handguns in their cars, looking for me. One had shot a chimney pot, so the armed police came, and this is what kicked off the Redworth riots: me taxing them! This in turn led to them carrying guns

139

BRIAN COCKERILL

while looking for me and then the police became involved and it escalated!

Firemen were being petrol-bombed, the police were getting petrol-bombed, cars getting blown up, and this went on for about two or three weeks and my taxing them was what kicked it all off.

I was going to bray them for going to my house. I got two of them and gave them some lessons from the Brian Cockerill Anger Management School. When I brayed them all over, they realised what they had done, but the others were running about like Keystone Cops with guns, saying, 'Well, we are going to have to shoot him because we can't fight him.'

They were showing off, they were giving it the large as if they were some delinquent on *The Trisha Show*. That was another carry-on.

Then I went to see my friend Speedy, who was behind bars. But then he got out and we had parties all over Stockton and Middlesbrough. We were just ruling the fucking roost, running all over, taxing the odd one here and there. People would just say, 'Brian, if we give you money, will you look after us?'

They would give me £100 and you might get 20 people paying you that. You were not selling drugs in competition with them, but you were not taxing them either, so they were paying you not to tax them. You were getting two grand a week for doing nothing, but you would just waste your money. You would go out and have a mad party and everyone would be off their heads and you would have just spent £1,200.

I would just give it away as if I was daft. You do this because when you were a kid you had nothing. It makes you spend money like water. There are people, snotty fuckers, who have been brought up with money, and they seem to be able to keep their money better than people who have been brought up on council estates.

140

THE NUMBER ONE TAX MAN

I was with Speedy and others, and Speedy was doing some bits and bobs. There was this lad who was said to have been selling heroin coming in from Nigeria. He came into town and was trying to sell it to someone and I was supposed to have gone to meet him at the Ladle pub. I was supposed to have bought half a kilo of heroin from him for 50 grand, or whatever the mad rumour was. This China light heroin had just come out in 1992. I was supposed to have pulled a handgun on him and said, 'Give me your fucking drugs.'

Thomo was in the car with me and I was supposed to have robbed this dealer at gunpoint.

Later, I was at home watching *Captain Scarlet* on telly when, all of a sudden, armed police were saying through a loudhailer, 'The building is surrounded.'

It was like a big kid's game. I thought, Not again!

Then I thought, The cunts might have put something there! I looked out of the window and the police were in jeeps, which they had only just started using. They were putting yellow tape everywhere and there were all these people in the middle of the street watching.

I should have just stayed in the house for a day or two and made a siege out of it. I was clean, I didn't have anything and I hadn't done anything. They had got it all wrong. But I came out, and I deliberately had no top on, to show them that I had no firearms on me, otherwise they could have shot me and said I had a weapon concealed about my person! The cunts had done it to plenty of people. There was one not so long ago with a wrapped chair leg in his hand and the police said it was a gun!

I lay on the ground and I was arrested and taken to the police station, where I was charged with armed robbery. Now, when you are put in an identification parade, there has to be an independent inspector from a different police station to supervise everything. But they are all the fucking same, so it's a load of bullshit. They arrange a line-up of people or they put you on a video line-up, or they can do a one-to-one confrontation with an alleged victim, but it has always got to be overseen by an independent inspector.

My solicitor came in and we were talking and the next thing was the police were saying I had put this handgun to the lad's head and taken the drugs off him. What happened is the lad got the deal off someone from a big, powerful firm and he was too frightened to go back to them empty-handed because they might have fucking killed him or something. He would rather have gone to the police and said he was a drug dealer and told them I had taken it off him than go back to these people.

One of the coppers had said to me, 'He's blaming you for taking a kilo off him and you've only taken half a kilo.'

'No comment,' I replied.

So, whether he was keeping half for himself and blaming us for half or whatever, I was nicked for armed robbery.

'Well, I haven't fucking done it,' I said.

I was sitting there on the ID parade. Weighing about 23 stone, of course I was going to look different, but my solicitor had said, 'Look, Brian, if it was Mickey Mouse in there, they are still going to pick you, know what I mean? They are going to blame you today!'

So, I was sitting there with a face like a twisted pretzel, deep in thought. I am going to get done for fuck all, I was thinking. The next minute the lad came in, and I had never seen him before in my life. The independent inspector started laughing and the sea of police faces around me fucking dropped. Somehow, they had jumped the gun with this inspection, because at first they had said it was a blue Cosworth I was in and then they said it was a white Cosworth and then they said I had tattoos up my neck. They hadn't corroborated anything!

This fucking drug dealer was not charged. It seemed the police were quite prepared to let the lad go free and continue with his little drug empire just so they could get me convicted and sent away for a long, long time! That is apparently how they police our streets! He was given immunity from conviction because he was the first person to give evidence against Brian Cockerill.

All in all, I never got charged. But it was on the local news and in the papers; the police were telling everyone I was an armed robber! They never put a correction in the paper the next week or ever said, sorry we were mistaken, it wasn't him.

One time I was driving down the motorway with my mate Flea. We had been to Hartlepool and there I had a fight with this lad and brayed him in the High Street over something. Out of the blue, a full police squad car pulled me over.

'We believe you have got drugs in the car,' the obviously armed copper said.

They searched the car. Nothing! My car and house have been turned over by the police for drugs and firearms many dozens of times, but they never got anything!

Another time I was staying at Flea's house. I'd been driving around in a Porsche with this girl that I was seeing and about five o'clock in the afternoon I pulled up outside and saw all these people in the street. I knew something was up when there was a sudden influx of window cleaners who didn't know how to clean windows properly! Somebody else was sweeping the path. It turned out they were all coppers, just as I thought.

'Brian Cockerill, get out of the car!' one of them shouted.

I was like, 'Put the fucking firearms away, you fucking idiots!'

I got out of the car and they said, 'We're going to arrest you on suspicion of drugs.'

Some fucking knobhead had said I was carrying drugs in the car. It was just bullshit. Pleasantries exchanged, they were ready to take me in.

I said, 'Listen, you go in my fucking car. I'm not sitting in yours and if you are driving mine I want to see your hands, as you could be planting something!'

I made them put their hands up so that I could watch where they were putting them. I didn't want them 'accidentally' dropping any drugs in the car.

When we got to the police station, a particular copper – he is an inspector in Thornaby now – had a hard-on to get me. They wanted to search my car at the station.

I said to this particular copper, 'I'm watching you fucking search my car and, when you're finished, give me the keys so that I can lock it so there is nothing planted in it, because some of the police have been vermin.'

There seems to be so much corruption in Teesside Police, it is unbelievable!

Then I went into the room and took my clothes off, underpants down and all that shit, so they could search me.

I had a little hole in my socks and they said sarcastically, 'What are you making now, Brian, 10 grand, 20 grand a week?'

'Look, I can't even afford a decent pair of socks,' I retorted.

When I was released and I drove the Porsche out of the police station, I remember wheel-spinning the car and making fucking smoke all over the place, just to annoy them. They were fucking devastated that they had nothing on me.

One night I knocked out this fucking doorman in Madison's nightclub, then I went on to a pub and Chubby Brown's son was there. There were these lads from London, a big firm, and they were very vociferous and jumping about, and then they all started fighting.

'Fucking sit down,' I told them, and half the fucking pub sat down.

The London firm said, 'They know who the governor is up here.'

With the London lads, we went on to certain pubs and the

doormen at one place tried to stop us getting in. One of these lippy cunts, who had a face like a smacked arse, said, 'You lot are going to have to pay.'

I was starting to look like a mug in front of the Londoners, so I dropped two of the doormen like used nosewipes and left them lying like crumpled paper. I looked at the third doorman and saw his foot move, which meant he was ready to throw a punch. I hit him about four times and he was still standing! He should have been a flatliner. I thought, He is not going down! What had happened was he was stuck. The door behind him was keeping him upright as I hit him like a steam train coming off the tracks! I broke his jaw and nearly killed him.

One of the London lads had bought me a big, two-ounce, gold boxing glove and I had it on a bracelet. I also had a Bunny Girl with a diamond in it and it was worth a bit of money. When I hit those blokes, I lost the lot, so I stopped wearing jewellery when I went out. Rings are especially dangerous if you hit someone – especially dangerous for you.

I didn't just tax drug dealers. There were a few times when I taxed the people putting on raves, because raves were a den of iniquity, a drug seller's paradise. At one time, the Robb brothers, Jimmy and Gary, came down to this area. They were doing a rave in Sunderland and they came down in T-shirts and got a place down here, on Norton Road, Stockton. It used to be called Henry Africa's, but that was shut down, and they opened it up as the Colosseum. It was nice, it was good, and they brought a lad down from Sunderland called Ernie Bewick to look after them.

I didn't know Ernie, but Thomo did because he used to go to raves in Sunderland. He said, 'He's a nice lad, Ernie. You should go and see him, Brian. He is sound.'

I said, 'Them cheeky cunts trying to bring people down, no. Cheeky cunts coming down here, Jimmy and Gary Robb, trying to open a rave and not fucking paying me.'

I fucking went to outdo them. I was foaming! They came down the first night and I just stood outside the place. There was brutal menace in the air.

I said to the punters, 'You're not going in!'

I wouldn't let anybody in, and Gary Robb only had about 30 people in on the first night they opened and no cunt would come in past me. A few went in with people they knew, but no Teesside people went in. It was knackered and a week later I got a phone call to go down and see Gary at the club.

I said, 'Nobody goes in.'

I went in and this group had come in and Gary said to me, 'This is Ernie.'

Out of all the top fighters I have met, I felt most relaxed shaking Ernie's hand. Ernie could fight for fun and beat all the top fighters, like Billy Robinson. Viv Graham was very wary of people like Ernie, as the lad could fight and he was a nice man. He was genuine, not like Lee Duffy, who would throw a punch and hit you when you had lowered your guard. Ernie wasn't like that at all.

We started talking and we had a bit of fun and then we sat down with Jimmy Robb, and Ernie said, 'Well, how much do you want then, Brian? I am just getting a wage out of it, but this is your area.'

I said, 'No problem, Ernie. Look, just give me £1 for every cunt that comes in.'

The next minute Ernie was talking to the Robbs and it was agreed. They would charge something like £10 entry on the door. A week later, I had 2,000 people in there and so I was on two grand on a Saturday night. Friday night wasn't as good, but I was still making about £1,000.

Ernie said, 'Watch these two lads, because they are scumbags.'

What happened is they put everything in their manager's name. He was a big fat guy; I can't remember his name now.

They tried to use the two of us to stop all the trouble, which we did, because nobody farted unless we gave the say-so.

Jimmy went away on holiday, I think, and Gary got jail for a few months and we just took the club and threw them out through the door. I said, 'Do you want the good news or the bad news?'

They said, 'What's the bad news?'

'The bad news is that we own the nightclub now!'

'What's the good news?'

'You've got fucking 20 minutes to leave!'

They fucked off, but a guy in Hartlepool owned the club, so we didn't have the power. When 200 police raided it in February 1996, it was all in his name.

This guy said, 'So you take the club with us, it's in my name, it's my club.' So the rave band QFX came in that night and the door receipts were 25 grand. After we paid all the staff and QFX and everything, we didn't earn a fortune; it was a few grand each. We made sure we paid everyone, but a week later they shut the fucking thing down.

In 1997, Gary Robb fled to the Turkish Republic of Northern Cyprus after facing drug charges. Northern Cyprus has no extradition treaty with the UK, because of its illegal status. It's the place where Asil Nadir, of the multi-billion-pound crashed company Polly Peck, escaped to. Mind you, Asil claims Turkish citizenship. Gary Robb, on the other hand, doesn't!

Facing the same charges as his brother was Jimmy Robb. He got 12 years for allowing the club to be used for the supply of ecstasy and amphetamines. The Robb empire had stretched from Berwick to Teesside. Now all of their clubs were put into receivership.

In an effort to keep his head above water, Gary Robb needed money sent over to him. In April 1999, Colin Thomas of Middlesbrough made arrangements to send him £100,000, but he was caught and sentenced to two years in prison.

In the meantime, I was, allegedly, opening a club called Dead Well. A man I mentioned earlier, Don Lorosh, had the club with me. Don had had one of the first rave clubs, the Eclipse. We opened another one called the Heaven Club, but the council came and read the rulebook to us. It was a members-only club and you had to be a member for at least 24 hours before you could get in, like a casino.

The punter would come in with some ID, say a passport and photographs, and would have their membership card stamped. The police sat outside, but I noticed they didn't sit outside Jimmy and Gary Robb's clubs and clubs run by all the other fucking scum. It could have had something to do with me, obviously! They sat outside the club every single night it was open and it was open three nights a week: Friday, Saturday and Sunday.

They sat out there from when the doors opened until the club shut just to intimidate people not to come in. I got the fire brigade to come and they gave the club a fire-safety certificate. When the council inspected it, they said it was one of the nicest-looking clubs in the town.

All the floors were done and upstairs it was like heaven, with all these angels, and downstairs was done out to look like hell. There was a drawback: we couldn't sell alcohol, only Coca-Cola and other soft drinks. Business never picked up because it was a small nightclub, not a massive club like the Colosseum. What fucked it was that the Colosseum was still open and everyone was used to going there. Besides, nobody dared to come because they were scared of me! We had good fun and it was a good club, but it lasted just six months and by then we had lost too much fucking money, so we shut down.

In the meantime, two friends of mine were approached by Jimmy Robb, who wanted ten kilos of blow off them. They give him his ten kilos, but about an hour later they got a phone call saying the gear was no good, 'So you can come and pick it up.'

When they went to the Colosseum to pick it up in his car, they drove down the street and got chased by the police. The lad who was driving, my mate, was a really good driver and they got away and put the gear in a beck and then drove home. When they got home, the police stung them, but they had no gear in the car. They were Newcastle Police, miles from their patch. What the fuck were the Newcastle Police doing in Teesside?

My mate Thomo was in the Colosseum and they asked, 'Thomo, how are you getting home?'

Thomo replied, 'I was going to pop home and come back.'

'Take my car,' he was told.

I asked Thomo why he didn't suss anything was wrong. He is not as quick as me, and if I'd been offered the Robbs' car I would have sussed them out. Anyway, Thomo took the car and the police stopped him as he was leaving the club and found under the seat what was at first thought to be 200 Es. It turned out that the tablets were ketamine. A legal substance, this is a non-barbiturate, rapid-acting dissociative anaesthetic used on animals and humans; it also has been used in human medicine for paediatric burn cases, in dentistry and in experimental psychotherapy. It is being abused by an increasing number of young people as a 'club drug' and is often distributed at raves. Hence the tie-in to the Robb brothers.

Ketamine is made into a tablet form by evaporating the liquid and reducing it to a fine white powder, and clubbers usually smoke or snort it. Often, because of its appearance, it is mistaken for cocaine or crystal meth.

'Bastard,' said Thomo, recalling how he had been set up. As he came out in the car, he got no further than a poxy ten feet and the police had him.

He told me another story about how the Robbs put a gun in a lad's car and set him up for the police. Just scumbags, they were.

I didn't find this out until later on, when I met the big fat manager after I took the club off them, but the crime squad went to see Jimmy and Gary and said, 'Let Brian Cockerill come in here, get him to see me.'

I rarely went out with my car but, if I did, I had a driver in a second car. I paid the driver to take the car home at night because I knew the tricks of the police. They would search your car if you were out in it, so I was playing safe.

'Fuck you,' I said, and never put anything in the car.

Anyway, what happened is that they said, 'We want to set Speedy and Brian Cockerill up' and 'We'll have them three cunts.' There was somebody else with me and Speedy that night, another lad from Teesside.

When they can't do you fairly, they will do you sneakily. The Robbs were trying to lull me into a false sense of security, trying to draw me in, but I was too clever for them. The things I was doing, I was too smart for the fuckers; they were as transparent as clingfilm.

I taxed one of their relations who worked for them when I took money off Jimmy McConnell. I had some Es for him to sell and took two grand off him. I also took something from somebody else of theirs, and then I found out that they were grassing. They weren't my cup of tea and the money I was making was good, so I decided it wasn't worth going to jail for that pair of scumbags.

They were from Berwick and weren't very well liked. When they wanted to get a firm together, they tried to get somebody from Newcastle to shoot me and then they tried to get somebody from Manchester to shoot me. I got a phone call from one of the big firms from there and then they went to Liverpool and I got a phone call from them and then they went to London and I got a phone call from there and then they ended up going full circle back to Newcastle and the lads said, 'Yes, we'll do it for you.'

The Robbs took them on the drink for the day and the Newcastle lads said, 'We're just going to make a phone call,' and then another lad came in and brayed the brothers with baseball bats for trying to get me done. And that was the end of Jimmy and Gary Robb. They are finished.

I never set it up; the lads did it because they like me, because I had done jobs for them before. And now Gary is on the run from the police. Jimmy tried to get doormen, but nobody wanted to work for them. He went to Eddy Ellwood and Denny Oyle and that pair of cunts worked on the door for them.

Ernie was as game as a pebble. He went to Eddy's gym and said to them, 'Well, you are going to get fucking battered.'

He wanted to fight them, but I said, 'They'll grass us up,' because I know their stamp. They are the type that will run with the moles and, as soon as there is any trouble, they will crash. Their strength is the police. They had been fighting in the street and knocked kids' teeth out and then they grassed them and took them to court, so they are not fighters.

It was rumoured that they wanted to fight me and, allegedly, I went down to the Colosseum to have a fight with them, but someone phoned the police on me, and I know it wasn't Eddy or any of his lot.

They were determined to shoot this cunt. And then another shooting took place in the street and people said, 'But it was never on the telly or anything.'

The police couldn't control it, they couldn't find the person who was doing the shootings – three in a fortnight. They were devastated. Nobody was saying anything, so they had hit a dead end.

I was nicked for both shootings in the club and then for making threats on a payphone. How the fuck can you get nicked for threatening someone on a payphone? I was supposed to have phoned Jimmy Robb and said, 'I'm going to shoot you, you daft cunt.'

While I was in court, I saw Graham Brown and Craig Beer, the best solicitors in Teesside, and they had been brilliant in getting me off charges.

Some of the things were true, but some of them were so far-fetched, the police trying to get you so much jail, they were ludicrous. They were saying that I had attempted to murder two coppers! In reality, all I was doing was driving my car. I was supposed to have gone at them in the car and then driven off.

My solicitor asked, 'How can it be attempted murder when he didn't even strike the vehicle, never mind the officers?'

They got me for dangerous driving, just pathetic things like that. Anyway, this Jimmy and Gary Robb got these two muppets to work on the door.

Ernie was going to bring 60, 70, 80 lads down here. Now, who was going to bash the fucking shit out of them all? Eddy Ellwood the body-builder and only about 20 other muppet doormen? They are not violent, and these lads that were with me just wanted to go in and shoot the lot of them!

The police got Ellwood and his lads bullet-proof vests and were escorting them to the gym and home every night. That's what big hard men they were, taken to the gym by armed police every day, and this went on for months.

I was taken to court and given bail. The charges sounded bad but they were pathetic. I was nicked for two shootings at the Blue Monkey, but at the time of one of them, I was in Stockton, in the High Street, and I passed a police officer where the bank was when the shooting took place at three o'clock, so he was my alibi. They were annoyed that I had a policeman for my alibi.

At the time of the other shooting, I was in a police station reporting that I'd lost my driving licence. I was on the camera there when the second shooting took place, so that was my other alibi. They were fucking fuming over this. They must have thought, This fucking clever cunt!

We went to court but they had to drop it all.

Then there was the time when I was working at the Blue Monkey for Jimmy and Gary Robb and they said they would give me £1 for every person that came into the club. They said I had threatened them, saying, 'I want £1 a man, I want so much money, blah, blah, blah.'

I asked the big fat manager, 'Why was I working there for six months until I was arrested? Why didn't they get me straight away? Why didn't they tell you, then, because you were setting me up?'

He said, 'They were going to put something in your car, obviously, Jimmy or Gary Robb, or put something in your clothes, your top or something like that.'

The problem with them putting something in my clothes was that I always wore a T-shirt and didn't wear a coat. I had this T-shirt that said on the front, 'The Number One Tax Man'.

One time the police arrested me and one of them said, 'Brian, what is that T-shirt with "The Number One Tax Man" on?'

I said, 'What are you on about?' and 'No comment!'

The copper asked, 'Well, then, can you tell me who "The Number One Tax Man" is?'

'The Chancellor of the Exchequer,' I replied. 'He lives in Downing Street, London.'

They were furious.

That time I'd been arrested by this copper Detective Inspector Russ Daglish, who, along with Detective Constable Brendon Whitehead, was accused of stealing a central heating boiler. Their fucking trial collapsed after wasting £½ million of taxpayers' money. It was slowed down when Chief Superintendent Pitt, who was welfare officer for DI Daglish, produced a huge report at a late stage of the proceedings.

I am just showing you the way the law works, as some of you actually believe the law to be beyond reproach. The very same Chief Superintendent Pitt, who in 1997 headed the Operation Lancet inquiry into claims of widespread corruption within Middlesbrough Police, which levelled 400 criminal allegations against 60 officers at a cost to the public of £6 million, was lambasted by Judge Richard Henriques, who told him he had 'shown absolutely no regard for the criminal justice process'.

Anyway, Detective Inspector Daglish, with about 20 coppers, arrested me at my house.

'The lad that was in the house with me had a scanner and he said, 'What shall we do now, Brian?'

The police were petrified; they wouldn't pull me in the street until there was an ARV (Armed Response Vehicle) on the scene. This copper had arrested me but I was adamant: 'I'm not going.'

The ARV turned up and eventually I got in the car with them and he said, 'Oh, Brian ...'

But I didn't give him a chance, telling him, 'Don't start talking a load of fucking shit, because I'm not interested in your fucking shit. I don't even want to talk to you!'

They took me to the police station and there I was as nice as pie, like I had been to some charm school en route. I was speaking nicely, I was polite during the taped conversation. You don't want to sound like a scumbag on the interview tapes, saying, 'Fuck this fucker.'

I just calmly said, 'No comment.'

For a second time I was asked, 'Who is this "Number One Tax Man"?'

I never batted an eyelid as I replied, 'I've already told you that,' then added, 'You're casting aspersions on my good name. I'm a pillar of society.'

Wearily, Daglish asked me, 'Well, yeah. So how did you know we were coming? Was it because of the scanner?'

I held his gaze as I said, 'There you go again, just jumping the gun. If you had asked me and taken the time, I would have told you that it wasn't tuned into any police rigs whatsoever. That device was tuned into the local aeroplanes, the airport, and that was my friend. That's got nothing to do with me.'

You would not believe how this incident came about; my Cosworth had been stolen from my house. A lad from Newcastle stole it, but I didn't know this until later on. Steam was coming out my ears! Every thieving cunt that had ever looked possessively at the car when I had it got a good hiding. I was just braying people like it was going out of fashion; every cunt was getting brayed.

This woman came up to me and pointed to a picture in a magazine. 'Are these the wheels and tyres?' she helpfully asked.

Well, they looked the same, so I said, 'Yes.'

She pointed to a nearby house and said, 'He's got them down there.'

I kicked the lad's door off the hinges and brayed the cunt all over the house. He managed to get a few words out in between me doing him in: 'Get out! They're the wrong tyres and the wrong wheels!'

Fucking hell, I guess the woman was only trying to help: she had a grudge against the poor cunt! Anyway, he was a tea leaf, so he deserved a doing over – allegedly, of course! When I went over there, I lost a gold ring as well – another reason not to wear jewellery.

My car had been stolen when I was in bed. I heard this noise and I thought it was the woman next door coming in. Obviously, they didn't know it was my house. Later, I found out where these toe-rags were from and I was going to break their arms and legs because they had been running around in a big white Cosworth. People had heard them saying, 'It's as fast as fuck.'

Oh, they also got £2,500 in cash that I left in it. I knew

it was them, so I went to get them, but on that very day they got five years apiece for robbery. So to this day, I've never got the cunts!

I was driving around council estates in Stockton on a Sunday afternoon like something out of *The Good, the Bad and the Ugly*. I was kicking doors in. I was looking through all the windows and the little peepholes and nobody was coming out because I was just braying every cunt, saying, 'Come here, you cunt, where's my car?'

A man came up to me near Ragworth, the roughest area, where they pinch cars and burn them out every night, and he went, 'I wish you were patrolling these areas instead of the police. I've had the best sleep ever in my life. In these last three nights there's been no robberies, no houses burgled, been no cars stolen. You would be 100 times better than the police. I would rather pay you than the police.'

The A–Z of criminals in the whole area had come to a standstill; everyone had just laid down tools. Nobody was buying drugs, all the pubs were empty and this went on for about two weeks.

I wouldn't even report the car stolen, that is how much I fucking hate the police, because they are just so horrible to me. I couldn't give a fuck. I don't need those cunts, I'll do it myself, I thought. I made it my sole enterprise to go out battering the lowlife scum. Decent people had no worries.

Now the police had got wind of me being on the warpath and lay in strategic wait. I went to this house and I was asking this lad about my car when this woman came out. I could smell the filth straight away. She was a plainclothes copper!

I said, 'Fuck off, I don't want to talk to you, now fuck off!'

My mate Bam Bam was with me and he, allegedly, picked a brick up and said, 'I'll fucking brick you, copper or not!'

And that is what led to them coming to arrest me. I didn't

threaten any copper with a brick, I just used foul language. We got in the car, drove round the corner and the next minute, a full squad car was going after us. I say 'squad car' but it was only a little red car.

When I was interviewed they said, 'Well, you must know what a police officer looks like?'

But the woman had been in plain clothes and I said, 'Of course I do, it's a bloke with a big fucking thing on there,' pointing to my head, 'with a truncheon and they've got police on their badge, you know what I mean! I'm not a mind reader, I can't tell when a plainclothes copper is a copper!'

I'd smelled the filth a mile off, but I was not going to give him the pleasure of knowing that, plus I had not done anything other than swear.

He was beginning to get aerated now and he said, 'Well, you know what a police car looks like.'

I said, 'Of course I do, it has got a big blue light on the top and a big red thing on the side and it says "Police" on the side of it. But when it's an unmarked police car, then it looks like any other car on the road.'

The copper was biting and biting. He was fuming. Then I was charged with threatening to beat up police officers.

I said to the copper, 'All I did was say, "Fuck off, I can't be arsed with you." Yes, swearing and telling them to fuck off is an offence and I am guilty.'

They still took me to court for it. The charge against Bam Bam was dropped. I'm not saying he was a bad one, because he isn't, but what I am saying is that his charge was dropped because they weren't interested in him; they only wanted me.

I was 'Target One' to them, but to me I was 'The Number One Tax Man'! They used to keep calling me 'Target One'. You could hear them on the scanner: 'We've got Target One' or 'We are looking at Target One.'

I remember, before I got nicked for this carry-on, in Teesside Park they had a full squad after me. My mate Spud was stopped because he had the same type of car as me, a Cosworth.

The copper was heard on the scanner saying, 'Approaching Target One' and this and that. Another copper came on the scanner and said, 'I don't think it is Brian Cockerill driving, though, you know,' to the other daft cunt.

On being told this, I phoned my solicitor and said, 'Listen, this lad has told me on the grapevine they are going to arrest these lads and they are waiting for them coming out of the Teesside bowling alley and the lads could get shot, as the law believe I am among them and they're waiting with an ARV. I'm not even there.'

So Craig phoned the police and told them and they came over the scanner and said, 'It's not Mr Cockerill. If you are out there, Mr Cockerill, you are listening to every word we are saying.'

Another time, a copper was whizzing down the road in Stockton and I was driving my car with a couple of mates and one was supposed to have had a scanner in his car. That was Paddy Watson, who is dead now, God rest his soul. The next minute I flashed my headlights at the copper.

Over the scanner, we heard him say, 'Brian Cockerill has flashed me in a Ford Sierra Cosworth.'

They told him, 'Pull up and wait for an ARV. Don't approach him, and lock your car door.'

Something else came on and I said to Paddy, 'What did that sign say there?'

'Forty miles an hour,' he told me.

I said to the copper, 'You're doing 60 mph. Keep your fucking speed down.'

I'd pulled the copper for speeding, and soon it was all over that the police had been breaking the speed limit.

Another day the police were following me everywhere, even undercover coppers. In retaliation, I started following them and they really got scared. Everywhere they went I followed them and this went on for about 30 minutes.

Then an armed squad car pulled me over and they asked, 'What are you doing?'

Calm as a cucumber, I answered, 'I'm chasing him, playing tuggy. If he follows me or you follow me, I'll follow you.'

That really rattled them; they didn't like it. They must have thought I was gone in the head! It wasn't that I wasn't right in the head. All of them are like Daleks, they're all the same. Everything they say is the same, whether you get nicked in Newcastle, Manchester or Liverpool – it's all bullshit. It's like McDonald's: it's the same the wide world over.

But getting back to that lad Micky Flanagan I was talking about in the previous chapter, the one who owned the gym where I trained. One day he said, 'Come on in, Brian. Come into the office.' The plot, I discovered later on, was to entice me in just long enough so that the police could fit a tracking device to my car. When I was in the office, he was somehow going to give the police the keys to my car. My mind still boggles at the thought!

The police thought I was in cahoots with the black lad from Leeds, who is now dead but who was a drug dealer doing heroin, but all I had done is phone his firm and threaten them that there would be war if they came down here and after that we never had trouble with them.

I went and saw my mate Kev Kilty, who knew a lad – Dave, you called him – who had a spy shop in Leeds called I Spy. I was staying at a flat with Kev and going in for Britain's Strongest Man. I was about 22 stone, and Kev was about 17 stone. I was driving down the motorway with Kev when I finally got done for driving offences.

The police had failed to do me for the shootings but now they sent armed officers after me and nicked me for dangerous driving. It's easy to think I am exaggerating the seriousness and consequences of armed police officers being on the loose, but, when you see the statistics for how many unarmed people they have killed, maybe you will understand my concerns.

Look at the way armed police have been criticised by the Police Complaints Authority for the way they handle incidents involving disturbed individuals. A report revealed that out of 24 cases of people being shot by armed police, 11 were trying to commit suicide. Well, I don't fall into that category. In one case, an armed officer is reported to have gone drinking the night before an early-morning raid!

Just take a look at the controversial shooting of James Ashley by coppers from Sussex Police in 1999. The man was naked and unarmed when he was shot dead! Police marksman Pc Chris Sherwood was cleared at the Old Bailey of the unlawful killing of Mr Ashley.

When they came for me, the police were all armed to the teeth with weapons of every description. They're going to try and shoot me, I thought, so I sped off in the Cosworth and they chased me like banshees!

I got away from the 17 police cars involved. Two of them blew up and one hit the pavement. I drove fucking excellently, and afterwards they said, 'It was the best bit of driving in the 40-minute chase.'

I was doing speeds in excess of 130 mph on 30-mph roads! I ended up in Darlington. To cut a long story short, I pleaded guilty to dangerous driving and was sent to prison for two years, plus three months for assaulting a police officer.

What led to the assault charge is another story. An Asian taxi driver, a big lad, the best fighter in Stockton until I beat him, had two of his radios stolen out of his taxi. I was with a lad from Grovehill called Basil and another mate of mine,

John, when the Asian lad came and demanded, 'I want them fucking radios!'

They were arguing and John hit the Asian lad with a stick and split his finger. The lads told the Asian lad there were two kids in the house and he should show some respect, but he just said, 'Fuck the kids.'

He was about 17 stone, just a tiny fish. When he came at me, he telegraphed a punch, which I deftly sidestepped. I hit him with a jackhammer of a left hook, sending him sprawling to the ground like a broken lift. He was knocked clean out for about 40 minutes. They tried to bring him around with smelling salts but it didn't work.

I fucked off to my mate Frankie Atherton's, leaving the car round the corner. The police knocked on the door about three o'clock in the morning, so I went and hid, as best I could, in the loft.

The police said, 'Come on down, Brian. Come on down.' It was embarrassing, it was like *The Price is Right*. So I was standing in the loft and I jumped down and unintentionally bust a copper, then another one hit me on the head with a truncheon and a third grabbed my arm and fell down the stairs with me. He broke his watch and got a two-inch scratch. They nicked me and I got three months for it.

Anyway, when I was in for the driving offences, I said, 'Look, I was chased by armed police.' Not even able to lie straight in their beds at night, the police said, 'Well, you should have stopped.' You should have done this, that and the other, they said. What they say to the judge in his chambers is all hush, hush, but it perhaps went something like: 'Look, we've got this dossier on this man, he's dangerous and needs to be taken off the streets. We can't prove anything, but can we get him off the fucking streets and give him the maximum.'

So I was found guilty, but I was bailed for reports. They like to lead you into a false sense of security, make you believe that you are not going to prison and then they slam you when you go back to court for sentencing.

As I was about to return for sentencing, I had a car crash in which I hurt my back and was laid up as a result.

The judge went apeshit and said, 'If he doesn't get down here, I am going to send someone to the hospital for him.'

That is how much they wanted me off the streets. News reached me of the impending situation and I fucked off out of the hospital window and went to stay at my mate's in Great Broughton.

I was running about and one night I went to this nightclub, which I shouldn't have, and there was this big, Eddy Ellwood look-alike character there, this big fucking body-builder, umpteen times Mr Universe, weighing about 22 stone, jumping about, posing and thinking he was fucking brilliant.

Anyway, he came up to me. Boom! I hit him and he was finished early for the night. As I dropped him with a left hook, you could see his muscles rippling; he put on a wonderful show. It took about six doormen to cart him off – hopefully to some manure heap.

Another time I was in this nightclub with Robby Armstrong, Richy Horsley, Stevie Lancaster and a few others and this ex-army lad came up to me. He was about 17 stone and six foot three, about the same height as me, and he said, 'I'm a tester for people like you, I run five miles a day, I box, I do a bit of karate and I'm an expert fighter in weapons.' It was like, 'Hello, I'm the real Rambo!'

I got him a drink and this other lad gave him an E, so we were soon off our heads. We were talking and he must have decided that I was scared of him because I had got him a drink, because he said, 'I know I could beat you, Br...'

Bang! Goodnight, Mr Rambo! I hit him with a right uppercut

and dropped him to the floor like a hot brick. He was going to be a little sore when he came around fully, he was groggy, half-awake and half-knocked out and he mumbled, 'I was only joking.'

'So was I,' I said. 'Ha, ha!'

He was fucked and I booted him up the arse, and that was the end of the tester. I have had too many fights like that where it is all over in five seconds. I remember Ellwood's brother coming into the club. He was about five foot eight and about 18 stone – massive! I was on a curfew at the time and I had to be in every night by six o'clock. I'd gone to the magistrates with Craig Beer who was representing me after I was nicked for making a threat from a payphone, and I was given bail on the condition that I was home every evening by 6pm.

I had to go to a door or a window and show myself when the police came and they would turn up three or four times every night, the bastards. Sometimes, to piss them off, I would say I was in the shower or something and make them wait an hour.

The funny thing is I had to stay outside a five-mile radius of Stockton, but I lived at Ingleby Barwick, only four and a half miles from the centre of the town! So I was breaking bail conditions by keeping bail conditions. It was fucking ludicrous!

The following week, when I went back to the magistrates I said, 'Can I just say something? The last magistrate gave me bail conditions to keep five miles away from Stockton, but I live four and a half miles from Stockton.'

The magistrate laughed and said, 'A mile from the place would do.'

It was around this time that Ernie and I were thinking about braying the Robbs, but then we got a phone call saying they were setting us up. They had CCTV cameras all over the club and the place was always wired up to an audiotape recorder. If we had gone, we would have got nicked because the armed police were in there. But it all came back to bite the brothers on the arse. They were playing right into the coppers' hands by videoing themselves selling drugs and doing all their dirty deals in the club. They all got 12 years apiece in the end, as I have already told you.

To return once again to the story of the gym owner who was supposed to be a friend but helped the police put the bug in my car, he wasn't looking well and lots of people were saying he was losing weight. He had lost two stone in about six weeks. He was only five foot seven and at 14 ½ stone he had looked huge, but at 12 ½ stone he looked like a shadow of his former self.

As well as that, he wouldn't look into my eyes when I was talking to him. I could see he was frightened I was going to find something out. Then he cracked and admitted the whole plot. 'Look, Brian, they have got me to try and set you up.'

I said, 'All right, mate, and blah, blah, blah.'

Later on, there were rumours that he had got me a kilo of coke. It was said that I had got this coke from him and then he gave me 30-odd grand for it and I kept the 30 grand. So we got the cunt back – allegedly.

This Micky Flanagan, I lent him two grand when he was struggling, I looked after his kids at New Year and they stayed at my house. The coppers had said, 'We'll get your kids back for you,' but they never did; they will say anything.

When I came out of a pub, I spotted a gas van sitting nearby. 'They are coppers, them,' I said to Kev Kilty. 'If they're not coppers, they'll stay in the van when I walk up to it.'

As soon as I started walking towards the van, the van sped off. Afterwards, this happened loads of times. That day I went to stay at my mate Kevin's and parked my car in such a way that I could see it from the window. I was putting it on the pavement, but a couple of weeks later the council came and put up bollards there, apparently as part of the Pub Watch scheme, so I couldn't park there any more.

Kevin said, 'It's funny, I've had this pub for three years and you've been parking there for two weeks and all of a sudden they've put bollards on the fucking thing.'

It was like when I went to the gym in Yarm one afternoon with Brian Flaherty. I notice when things are different, and I knew that the car park held about 20 cars.

I asked, 'Do you notice anything different?'

He replied, 'No.'

'Well, we'll go into the gym,' I said.

Brian said, 'I'll just park my car in the middle of the rows for now and, when somebody comes out, I'll move it. They'll drive theirs out and I'll put mine in.'

We were sitting in the gym and I said, 'Don't you notice something in the gym?'

'What?' Brian said.

I said, 'There are only four people in the gym and there are 20 cars in the car park! That's because the police station is only about two streets away.'

He said, 'You're paranoid.'

I said, 'I'm not fucking paranoid.'

The fucking next thing, they had managed to bug the car, and Micky Flanagan had helped them do it. They wanted me to park down the street and that was why the car park was chock-a-block. Micky gave my girlfriend free tokens to the sunbed, so that kept her tied up. When I went in to the gym, I would hand my car keys over for safekeeping, and that is how the police ended up being able to put the tracker on my car.

The bug was a magnetic tracker, as big as a mobile phone, and was stuck beneath the car. I was going to get the brakes done the next day and I was looking under the car when I spotted it, so I prised it off.

I went to see Kevin and we set off for Leeds. I presumed that the police would think I was going to meet this black lad from Leeds, because he lived in that area. I spotted their cars following us. When I was being followed, what I used to do is drive at 100 mph, then slow right down to 30 mph. With those tactics, it wasn't hard to spot anyone following you, but of course a tracking device is different. You could travel at 1,000 mph and they would still eventually find you.

I used to pull into lay-bys and sit for half an hour and then turn back and go the other way, and they would be waiting for me down that way, but it allowed me to suss them out.

Anyway, we went through Bradford first and it was 'spot the white man'. I am not being racist, just telling it how it was. There were hardly any whites where we were and only one bloke who was obviously a copper. The fucking idiot was pretending to be looking at a map but he stuck out like a sore thumb.

I said, 'He's a copper, we've sussed him, and he knows that we have sussed him,' so I greeted him, 'Hello!'

We got to Leeds about half-four or five, parked and walked to Kev's mate's surveillance shop. They talked a bit and then Kev showed Dave the tracking device that I'd found on my car. Dave said, 'It's a really expensive one,' then took it apart and examined it closely. He told us, 'I've been in this game 25 years and it is the strongest battery [it was a long-life lithium one] I've ever come across. Every ten seconds it comes on and goes off after two seconds, it is transmitting at VH frequency, which is what televisions use. Unusual!'

This going on and off was to save the life of the battery, plus if you've got a bug detector it makes it more difficult to detect, as the bug is intermittently going on and off. The police knew I had bug detectors and similar equipment. Trackers are sophisticated pieces of kit and the lifetime of the one that was attached to my car could have been many weeks.

With that in mind, I would say that they wanted to locate me and set me up.

Besides, Micky Flanagan had already admitted, 'The police are just waiting for your car, they're down there now and they've put a tracker on your car. I didn't want you finding out it was me because you would get somebody to fucking shoot me.'

I said, 'I wouldn't do something like that. I would just take 30 grand off you later, you cunt, you know what I mean.'

I stayed friendly with him for another six months and then did him for 30-odd grand. Fuck you, I thought.

I could have just left the tracker on my car. I wasn't doing anything wrong. Even though Mick Todd had put it on my car, as coppers go he was all right, he was fair. I am not saying the other fucking one he was working with was, but Todd was fair in an old-fashioned way.

Dave in I Spy took a bug detector into my car to see if it was bugged, but it was clean. He came back, gave me the tracker and said, 'Put it in your pocket.'

I knew enough to know that the only people who buy that sort of thing wholesale are the National Crime Squad, the likes of MI5 and HM Customs. 'How much is something like that worth?' I asked.

'You're talking thousands,' he said. 'It's top of the range, that one. Have you been talking on the phone?'

'Yes,' I said.

Of course I had been on the phone. I thought, this is where the coppers are jumping the gun again, thinking I was looking for somebody. They followed me and I was in a Saab convertible, with a 17-stone lad next to me and another kid weighing 25-stone, well known to them. As if you would drive to fucking Leeds to get gear in your own fucking car, registered to you, and then drive back with it. You would have to be fucking daft, but that is how thick they are – stupid as fuck.

The police have carried out loads of undercover operations on me. They have even asked people I know if they could use their house to watch me. I know a girl who works in a police station as a cleaner and she told me, 'They've got a massive dossier as big as a house end on you, Speedy, Bam Bam and all the different people connected to you. They call it Operation Gorilla.'

Cheeky cunts, I thought. Operation Gorilla made me laugh, as I'm bigger than a gorilla! They should have called it Operation Mighty Joe Young, after the film.

So I put the tracking device in my pocket and I said to Dave, 'How much do I owe you?'

Licking his lips, he said, 'Get me a pint.'

We went into this nearby pub, from where I phoned my solicitor and said, 'Listen, we're going to get nicked on the way back from Leeds. Can you do me a favour and fax this serial number of the tracking device to various high places and take a note of the number I'm calling you from? If the police have us nicked and get us done for something they say we have done on the way home, then you have proof of where I have been.'

Now, how the fuck would I have the serial number unless I had had that transmitter in my hand, so I repeated, 'Will you fax it off to different places while I'm here because they'll only take the piss otherwise?'

When we came out, kids were running about and then suddenly there were fucking armed police everywhere; coppers with coshes running towards us. I saw four or five lads and Mick Todd was at the fucking back, shitting himself. The shitty arse was thinking, if I stay at the back he won't hit me. I was standing there and one of the coppers must have had a death wish as he came at me with a cosh.

'You hit me with that and I'll knock you into fucking tomorrow,' I raged. 'I'll break your fucking jaw for you and you'll need a check-up from the neck up! Now put the fucking thing down!'

I got on the phone to the solicitor, telling him what was going on. When I'd finished, they said, 'There's no use resisting arrest.'

You get three months shoved up you for resisting arrest, so I was just standing there, but none of them took liberties with me.

I said, 'You're not putting handcuffs on behind my back. I'm too big to start sitting like that all night, because you start getting stiff shoulders.' Then I warned them, 'There's no need for you coppers to be kicking off, because there is no trouble.'

All these armed police were lined up with their guns out and I could see by their intimidating look that they had itchy trigger fingers.

I said, 'Don't even think about the guns now because there are kids here.'

So Kevin was nicked, I was nicked and Flaherty was nicked. The police handcuffed me with two sets of the contraptions. They put me in the car and Mick Todd said, 'We've got you now, Brian. We have got gear in your car.'

I said, 'If you two are police officers, will you go over there with them because they are scumbag police. They are Operation Rancid, they have been fucking done for fucking taking drugs out of houses and fucking cutting it.'

Rumours on the street said that a copper I knew had been shagging a prostitute and had a lad working for him selling coke. The copper was getting the gear, cutting it up and giving his sellers a wage every week. When the coppers went into this house, they would say to the two girls there, 'Give us a line.' The word on the streets was that they were having lines of coke, that they were all taking it and they were going over the border and buying it off a lad.

A desk sergeant had apparently blown them up and this is how the investigation was sparked off. Some officers were reportedly doctoring the crime numbers by getting people they had caught for, say, burglary to confess to other burglaries they had not done. They were doing that with car crimes and other things too and people were agreeing to it, but then some of them said the police had given them drugs.

One of the lads dealing for the police phoned me and said, 'Brian, I've got some work. Will you get these lads to tax this lad?'

I knew the police had got on to him, so, if I had gone into the house and taxed him, taken the drugs off him, they would have nicked me with drugs on me. Naturally, I wouldn't be able to say I had just taken them off him. They were trying to set me up, knowing I would tax and get hold of the drugs. But I knew it was a set-up. They couldn't get me for taxing, but they would have got me for carrying drugs. I knew what they were up to, and that is why when I do taxing I only take money. They must have been so frustrated!

One time I was with my friends Paddy and Angus. We had been to Stockton and come back and, when I went into Paddy's house, about 20 undercover police steamed the place. They did it on suspicion that we had drugs in the house. I had £150 in my pocket, but there were no drugs in my car, no drugs on me and no drugs in my house, two miles away.

But Angus, after I dropped him off, got caught with about nine ounces of speed in his house. He said to the police, 'It's nothing to do with Brian, it's my gear. I sell the gear, it's mine. It's nothing to do with Brian and Paddy.'

Angus got two years, I think. What I am saying is they try and do you for anything.

I myself got nicked for drugs in somebody else's house two or three doors away. I was taken to court the next day and the police were going, 'We've got him, we've got him here.'

It was the same after they nicked us in Leeds. They were cocksure that they had something. But when they searched the car there was nothing! They took me in, but I was only held for two-and-a-half hours and then let loose because I had proof of where I was at and proof that they had put this illegal bug on my car.

They said, 'You're not meant to complain about that.'

When I said I knew it was illegal, and all about Operation Lancet, in which Teesside Police had been suspended, the officer, Mick Todd, was shitting himself, thinking, I'm going to be fucked here – another fucking allegation.

To cover his arse he said, 'Well, I had to bug your car because of the way you drive, you're too good a driver.'

I said, 'Stop fucking patronising me and bullshitting me!'

'We've got egg on our chin,' he admitted.

'No, you haven't, you've got a breakfast on your face. What a right fucking mess you've made!' I told him.

He said, 'We're going to let you go, son.'

I could hear this senior officer saying, 'You said that they had firearms, drugs and money. They've got nothing. They've got £150 between the three of them, the other one is falling to bits, Flaherty, because he is bad with his arm and bad with this and bad with everything.'

After that, he said to me about Flaherty, 'If he was your backup, you are fucked.'

I said, 'There's no backup because you illegally bugged my car.'

I have been in longer for a fucking parking ticket.

While they were holding me, the police in Stockton were sitting outside my house, anticipating a call to go in. They call that a 'knock' and, if they get one result there, they go through everything. It's the domino effect. One thing gets a result and it's boom, boom, boom! They go through the lot. It never bothers me because they know I don't do anything. I do the odd security now more than anything, but, when I went to jail in November 1995 for 27 months for the driving and assault charges, they breathed a sigh of relief.

I have already mentioned that while I was on bail awaiting

sentencing I went on the run. When the police finally caught up with me, I was in my mum's caravan in Saltburn. It was about eight o'clock in the morning and I heard this noise. Under the caravans and everywhere was a fully armed squad of police, in bulletproof jackets and all the other paraphernalia, all waiting for me.

I was nicked and taken to Redcar Police Station and from there to the crown court. I went in front of Judge Macdonald, who was a bastard. I was remanded into custody because the sentencing judge from my trial was on holiday.

In a fit of rage, I fucked my barrister off and got this new barrister called Les Spittles, who had a Teesside accent. 'You're going to get a big sentence, you know, son!' he told me.

While I was on remand, the lads were saying that I would get three months or so. There was another lad, up for 12 driving offences, and he got six months. Another one was done for 15 driving offences and got three months. When you compare it with what I got, two years and three months, it's fucking ridiculous.

While behind bars, I went on a car-offenders course. There were ten of us on it and I had the biggest sentence out of everyone, even though some of them had stolen cars or crashed cars and were in for three months.

The police had been working to get me behind bars for a long time, by hook or by crook. But my reign was far from over!

14 GOOD FELLAS

YOU WOULD THINK the police would be happy enough at me being behind bars for a paltry driving charge, but it was also deemed that, even in prison, I was a danger to the inmates and a danger to this and that. They did this to prevent me from being allocated category-D status, which would have meant I could have been transferred to an open prison. Instead, I was allocated the security status of a cat-C prisoner – semi-open conditions.

Just going back to my trial for a moment, when I was arrested and eventually put on the ID parade, the motorbike copper said, 'Cockerill was in the car and he had come out and said, "I will fucking knock you out, you black cunt."'

You have never seen anything like it in your life; they were like a load of kids in the courtroom. I thought, you big dozy cunt. It was like looking at an erection with ears when you looked at him; he had this big bald head. I looked at him and I thought, Well, no wonder they are all brain-dead with him on the case.

The motorbike copper was asked, 'How did you identify Mr Cockerill?'

He replied, 'Well, I went back to the police station and I looked at his file.'

Then he was asked, 'How did you know which file to pull if you didn't know who Mr Cockerill was?'

He was slowly being given the rope with which to hang himself. It seemed quite obvious, somebody had told him who I was.

The motorbike cop said, 'I recall the independent inspector said you have got to have photographic evidence, it has got to be on, like, a file.'

Judge Fox turned to him and repeated the question, 'How did you know which file to pull?'

Later, because of a hung jury, the case was kicked out of court.

So I came back for a retrial and Judge Scott let it go ahead. How can it be that one judge says no and the other one can say yes?

When I first went to jail, because of being on the run, I was in Holme House Prison in Stockton. But I was only there for a few days and then I went back up for my appeal against being remanded because I wanted to get bail. I went in on the Friday or Saturday and I was back at court on the Tuesday or Wednesday.

Before I went to court, I had a run-in with a lad called Chris Curry, who was the top man at Holme House; he was in for all sorts. This very same man, I had brayed him in Redcar a few years before, but in jail I didn't recognise him at first. I had gone into this house in Redcar because he was beating up and robbing drug dealers and they were paying him money to stop him from beating them up. I'm just telling you the background story so that you know the crack with him.

I went into the house with Speedy and I was looking about for my prey. No one was in, it seemed. But I had a few old tricks up my sleeve, like feeling how warm the car bonnet is, feeling the kettle, the bed and other things. The bed was warm and so was the kettle. He's in the house and can't be far away, I thought. I turned the electricity off so I could hear better. I could hear this breathing. Where the fuck is he?

Eventually I located the breathing to the settee. The cunt was hiding in the settee, which had a false bottom. He was a sitting duck! I dragged him out and gave him a heavy-duty braying. I was hitting him with such force that I ended up hitting myself in the fucking eyes! I nearly poked my eye out and then I lost the plot! The argy-bargy began and I floored him with a combination of TV sets, lamps, ornaments and anything else I could get my hands on. There was no escape for him. I threw him at the window – we were three storeys up!

Speedy pleaded, 'Brian, you're going to fucking kill him if you throw him out the window!'

By now I was intoxicated and exhilarated by my spectacular display of violence!

'So, fuck, I'll throw the bastard out the window!' I bawled.

I was trying to throw him out and Speedy was still screaming, 'Brian, Brian, you're going to fucking kill him, man!'

Somehow, I came to my senses. I didn't want to kill anyone, so I let him go. This lad didn't know who I was and he went on the run and fucked off.

I met my mate Jimmy in jail and he said that Curry was scared of me. The lads would give me bits and bobs, radios and batteries, and shit like that. A few of them said things like, 'This Curry was telling us about when he beat Brian Cockerill.'

Curry had the prison record for doing a 500-pound squat with the weights, so I did 500 just to take the piss. I destroyed the record and then did repetitions with 600- and 650-pound squats.

I'd been in there two days and he was telling me he was going to beat me up. He was just across the landing from me and he walked up to me and said, 'All right.'

'Who the hell is that daft cunt?' I said.

That's when it came to me that this Curry was the guy that had hidden in the settee. Although I had battered him, I never got a good look at him that day because he'd had thick-rimmed glasses on. He was a bigger-than-average lad, about 16 stone and five foot eleven.

These weren't just little lightweights that I was fighting. Some of the lads had been away for armed robbery and shooting people, stabbing people, sticking needles in people; one stuck a needle in a taxi driver.

Curry came up to me and said something like, 'Come on then, come on, you cunt!'

I thought, Don't hit him with your right hand on the chin or a left hook on the chin, just stick him in the eye, so I jabbed him. I hit him with a sweeping left hook that split his eye open like a gutted fish!

I was, 'Come on, you cunt!'

Everyone had seen it and was over the moon because he'd been bullying them all. So then I dropped him in this netting that was there to stop people throwing themselves off the high landings, so he didn't hit the floor.

By now it was mealtime and I went down with the other prisoners to the dining area to pick up our trays, be served and take our food to our cells, where we ate our meals. I was in this cell with this lad from Hartlepool. The doors had gaps down the sides and you could see through these. My pad mate was looking out, across to Curry's cell, and giving me a running commentary, 'He's got his light on and there are screws in with him.'

'Here,' I said, 'he'll be going around with a thing on his eye looking like Long John Silver.'

The screws opened our cell door and were very polite when they said, 'What it is, Brian, you are just going on the block, there's no trouble or anything.'

They were so nice about it, what could I do but go? I

accompanied them to the segregation block and there they asked, 'Well, what do you want to say about it?'

I said, 'Well, there isn't a lot to say really.'

So the screw said, 'Well, you've beaten him up, and, by all accounts, you've beaten him up before.'

He'd fucking grassed me right up, the cunt! They shipped me out: what we called 'ghosted'.

'We're shipping you out now because we don't really want you here,' they said.

I hadn't been there five minutes and I was barred from Holme House Prison! But the day before, when I was in the yard, there were 30 or 40 lads walking around with me, and when I sat down these lads were sitting there saying, 'Tell me when you had a fight with him,' and things like that. I was telling them stories. I was like the teacher telling the kids and they loved it, all the young lads.

So I was 'ghosted' to Durham Prison. When I got there, the screws told me how they hated the Currys. They sat me down, gave me a coffee and they were having a bit of a laugh with me. I had hoped they had forgotten about the riot I caused there in 1991. They were all right, as they go. When a copper nicks me and it is a fair cop, then fair enough, but what makes me angry is the dirty cunts who haven't got the brains to catch you and have got to set you up.

When I got remanded all those years ago I was on B Wing, and now I was in the same cell! I was in with this lad who was only in for poll tax, poor cunt.

'Are you all right, kid?' I said.

He was only in for a week and he was shit-scared and he asked, 'What are you in for?'

'Dangerous driving,' I said.

Everyone was saying, 'Can you remember when you got nicked for that shooting?' and all these fucking things. This poor kid was shitting himself, so I said, 'Don't worry about me, I'm not like that. Don't worry.'

Well, I wanted to get on to D Wing, because it was a remand wing and I was still officially on remand, although I was classed as convicted, awaiting sentence. On this remand wing, you were allowed £15 a week to spend at the shop and you were allowed to wear your own clothes. I got my way: I was sent to D Wing, still wearing my own clothes, even though you are supposed to wear prison clothes when you are convicted.

All of the screws wanted me on the wing because they knew I wasn't a bully. When I got there, I said, 'There's no fucking bullying in here,' because one of the lads had some sovereign rings and they were trying to take them off him. I went into the yard and I said, 'Any fucking bullying in here and I will be the fucking bully,' and that stopped it all.

The way I look at it is, you are all in jail, you are all having a hard fucking time, but you see young kids hanging themselves through people bullying them. I couldn't live with myself if I thought I could have done something about that but didn't.

Anyway, then I got fucking convicted. I think they were going to send me to Acklington Prison in Northumberland. I remember when Stevie and Michael Sayers came in, they had just got ten years each and I was walking around the yard with them.

They must have thought, all these top firms and he has got full control of everything, and so I got shipped out. But, when I was in there, I was all right and we had a good laugh. We used to go to the gym and also work on the bins.

I got shipped from there to Haverigg Prison in Millom, Cumbria. I had heard of black sheep and I thought it was just a saying: the black sheep of the family. There were only two of us from Durham Jail going to this place and we were shipped in this van, like a minibus, and when we arrived there were fucking black sheep and brown sheep running about on the hills.

GOOD FELLAS

I was in this jail in the middle of nowhere and it was all fucking metal: the gates, the building, the floor, the roof – everything was metal, though the windows were hard plastic. But the cells were spotless, better than Durham. The toilets flushed, there were radios and electricity in the cells.

I was in what they called the induction phase, sitting there in this little cell on A Side. Eventually you move to B Side, but first you are in A Side for so many weeks and the screws all watch you like hawks; they can see everything you are doing. You do get out and you can have a game of pool for an hour, but you are locked in your cell all day and it is freezing.

In this fucking cell, there were no radiators, but there was a big pipe that went all the way through the cells that was supposed to provide heating. These must have been the coldest prison cells on the planet. It was so cold that even the walls were shivering! I was fucking freezing and I had this donkey jacket on, but my legs were so big I couldn't get any jeans to fit me, so I was allowed to wear tracksuit bottoms. I could wear my sweatshirt too, so I was in there with all my own clothes on.

I was the only person, ever, in all the prisons I had been in, who was allowed to wear their own clothes: in Holme House, Durham, Haverigg and later at Walton.

One of the screws said, 'Is it cold in here?'

I said, 'Is it cold! There's two penguins and a polar bear under the bed.'

He said, 'The heating is broken.'

I was sitting, fucking freezing, for two days, then they put me in another cell and it was fucking boiling. It was like Bermuda: fucking waves and people on surfboards going by.

The place was full of Cumbrian people and there were a lot of Irish and Scottish and loads of Scousers. It was fucking chocker. I think it holds 600, 700 prisoners, but in the induction section – everybody called it 'the camp' – there were about 16 cells in

179

each block, though some have 10 or 12 cells. They lock the doors at each end and you have got your rooms and the bars on the doors. You could easily get out, but you couldn't go anywhere because it's in the middle of nowhere and the screws had to be brought to work in tractors because it was knee-deep in snow. It was so bad that the RAF were dropping the food in for the prison because they couldn't get it in by road. Some lads escaped, fools, and they had been out for nearly two days when they did an about-turn and knocked on the door to get back in because they were freezing.

There was no gym, fuck all to do there. I'd been messed about moving from jail to jail and now I was in this induction camp, sitting there and thinking about all the raves and girlfriends and all this shit. You might make a phone call, but that two-quid phone card only lasts two seconds for calls from there to Teesside.

The Cumbrians were, 'All right, la'?' and 'Got any shine?', meaning tin foil. They were like fucking locusts. A lot of the Scousers, not all of them, were a pain in the arse.

I got talking with a few of the lads, playing pool and shit like that. You were only out for an hour and you could walk around in this metal building, and you had to walk about a one-mile round trip to get your food, and that was your exercise. By the time you got back with your food it was stone cold.

I was only in there about five days but during that time I lost a bit of weight. I was still about 19 stone, though, bigger than anyone else.

There was this screw who was all right with people and he was going to this body-building thing every night as the prison was having a strongman competition.

Out of the blue, he asked me, 'Do you want to go?'

'I would love to go,' I replied.

He said, 'I'll get you in, kid. I know you are into training.'

I thought, Fucking brilliant! He was all right with me and he got me in, although you were not supposed to go if you were on induction. I was sitting contentedly in the crowd, and the next thing, a few lads had got this bench-press competition going. You had to do as many bench-presses as you could with this 60-kilo barbell. It wasn't a lot of weight. I was sitting there full of flu and the sweat was pissing out of me, and they were saying, 'Who's having a go?'

About four of them did. One lad managed 20 reps, another 45. Bear in mind there was no proper food in there, so the lads were doing all these reps on very little energy. There was one who used to be a Mr Universe; he got about 35 reps and somebody else squeezed 40.

I went on and got 77. They were fucking devastated and I was accused of being a plant, but that was one of the disgruntled body-builders. With the right food, I could have reached 200 reps.

I won a massive trophy. They had been training all year and when they came up to me I said, 'It's a nice trophy, isn't it?' I was buzzing because in there you have got nothing, you're sitting with nothing and then you go out and you win a trophy and they are all saying, 'He's only been here five minutes. Seventy-seven reps – he's strong, him.'

Everyone was talking about me, the one who had just come in the jail, 'a Geordie lad'. Even though I talk with a Teesside accent, to them I was a Geordie. Try convincing someone in Newcastle that anyone from Teesside is a Geordie and they will argue the point. But for the sake of peace I accepted the tag.

After two weeks, I was moved to Side B. I was in there for about six weeks, while every other cunt was going back on the camp and getting some sort of paying job. You have to work for money and this keeps the prison running smoothly. After two or three weeks of having no job, I thought I must have a red cross on my door and no fucker was allowed in or something.

I didn't get a job for ages, but in the end this bloke in the school said, 'I've been watching you, Brian, and you're a good lad. You're not a bully and you don't let other people get bullied. Would you like a job in the laundry? There's a place coming up and it's the best job in the jail because you get £9.29 a week and you get to wash your own clothes.'

I got this job in the laundry and, I fucking tell you, you worked. You had to wash 2,000 sheets a day: you would wash them and then put them in this thing called a carousel and they would go through and come out dry. When they came out, you folded them and then you did this and you did that and you got used to it.

There were perks: some of the lads wanted their stuff pressed or their collars and cuffs starched, or their gear washed in a hurry, and I got plenty of phone cards as payment.

You were washing for six football teams and six rugby teams for the local people and you were washing for three jails, 1,500 men.

I was in with this Scouser called Johno.

'What are you in for?' I asked.

He answered, 'I was with my mate and we were on the speed in Liverpool. He kept fucking bullying me all the time. So one night I went to his house and smashed his head in with a hammer and hit him 27 times with it and then put him in the car and took him down the tip and dumped him, but they got me, but at least I killed him.'

Before I went there, I was in Durham with another killer, but it didn't bother me. But you can imagine the poor cunts who are only in for car thefts, who are only normal people, and they would be terrified.

I met this lad from Durham and asked what he was in for and he said, 'Murder.'

You could tell he was a psychopath and I thought, I've got to watch this cunt, he looks like a loon!

Another killer was from Cumbria. Guns and knives and things like that fascinated him. He said, 'I had this crossbow and I shot my mate, but it only shook him a little bit. So I had a crossbow with a 150-pound pull there, and I shot it right through him and he dropped like a bag of shit.'

'Why did you shoot him?' I asked.

He replied, 'I just wanted to know what it felt like to shoot somebody with a crossbow!'

For that, he got life with a recommendation that he serve six years – not bad for killing someone just to see what it feels like.

A lot of people used to get a bit of blow and you would get your head down, but then they would come round for urine samples, which I thought was bad because people might have a bit of blow and it made you happy and got you to sleep and there was no trouble.

By doing these urine tests, they were driving people on to heroin. People don't take heroin usually when they're in prison. They have a bit of blow so they can get their head down on a weekend, get themselves mellow.

Cannabis resin is in your system for something like 30 days, so, if you get a piss test, you are going to get caught, so you only take a little tiny bit and you can sweat it out of you or whatever. But heroin is only in your system for 24 hours, so if you take that on a Saturday night – and they don't piss-test on a Sunday – you would be clear by the Monday, but the addiction process is fast.

If you are taking a bit of blow, it might not do you any harm, but if you start taking heroin you get addicted to the fucking thing, and people were getting addicted to it. Some people were having a go with it on a weekend, knowing it would be out of their system on Monday. And then they'd have another one and another one, and more and more people were becoming addicted to heroin. There was more heroin going through the jail than ever. If you took ecstasy, it would be in your system for four days, so you couldn't take that. You couldn't take sleeping tablets because they take two to four days. And you couldn't take cocaine because that is five days. Blow is 30 days, so there were loads of people in prison taking heroin and getting hooked.

I said all of this to a woman governor and she said, 'I have never thought of that.'

I said, 'People don't think of these things.'

Being in prison can open your eyes, and I am basically streetwise, but in jail you are talking to people in there you don't know from Adam. They are in for shooting and all sorts. Then there are fucking grasses working with the screws. It's all right talking to them, but I wouldn't go around grassing people up.

When I got the job in the laundry, I was moved on to 'the camp'. It was like staying in the Savoy in comparison to A and B Sides. You could watch telly and then you could go into your cell or into any of 16 different cells and talk to whoever you wanted to. You had kitchen facilities with a kettle. It was great.

You could go to the gym twice a day, so I started going. There was a screw there called Neville and another one whose name I can't remember. They were sound with me. I would do circuits. When I started off I could do press-ups and sit-ups non-stop for an hour.

There was a lad called Easty, a fucking small lad, only four stone, but he was superfit. There were 500 lads and they were only 12 or 13 stone at most. I was still superfit and usually third, fourth or fifth fastest on the circuits.

Even on a poor prison diet, I was still squatting and doing 400-pound bench-presses. I did loads of courses, as they all contributed towards points and points meant home leave! If you didn't do that, there was no home leave.

I thought to myself that being in jail was me being taxed for what I had done. I had done my taxing; now I was paying for what I'd done. I knew it was something I had to endure. I thought, Fuck going in the block all the time, getting locked up with a fucking lot of people. I had seen too many fellow cons kicking off and I know of some who have spent over 20 years in solitary. I consider them fools. I kept thinking, Don't hit another fucker because you are just going to get shipped out again and I had just got settled in there.

I had to show people my raw power, because by doing so I would be able to stave off trouble without throwing a punch at anyone. The best way to do it, I decided, was to put on a little performance. So I looked around the gym for someone of large build and spotted a Scouser.

I said, 'Here, mate, can you give me a hand?'

He was big lad, about 14 stone, and I said, 'Hold these pads for me.'

I put on the gloves and went on the punchbag to warm up before punching the pads held by the Scouser. I was going to have to make this the most impressive performance of my life! I used all of my old boxing skills to make the bag scream. By the time I had finished, the whole of the gym had gathered around to watch. I was on a voyage of destruction! I gulped in the stale gym air to fuel my muscles; my lungs were begging for more air. I drew on all the energy I could muster as I made the bag swing like a metronome.

When I stopped, I could hear gasps of, 'Fucking hell, if you hit someone with one of them shots you would kill some cunt.'

But my performance wasn't over yet. 'Are you ready with those pads?' I said to the Scouser.

I had my own pads and I did some elementary right hooks and some left hooks.

'Fucking hell!' he said.

'Right,' I said, 'hold them tight,' as I burst into a punching frenzy that I knew would have floored a rhino. My fists flashed in a blur of screaming leather and I punched like there was no tomorrow!

When I had finished, I could see that the jaws of most of the men watching had dropped to their knees. I had won a fight psychologically and I hadn't hit anyone. They had seen me on the bag and they thought, Fuck that for a game of soldiers!

This lad called Moxy said to me, 'You'll kill some cunt,' and then to someone else, 'Have you seen this fucker on the bag here?'

I used to be able to do ten two-minute rounds and then I could do six threes; twice a week I was doing that. I was doing everything to do with training and I was doing two big circuits a week, twice on the bag, twice a week in the bag room and then doing the weights during the week, six days a week!

For some reason they started called me Big Vern, like that character in *Viz*. That was my nickname in Haverigg. What I started doing is I got a lad working in the kitchens and he would get me some cheese and two pints of milk every day. The kitchen staff were entitled to get a bit of milk every day and in return I would give him a phone card every week.

I had somebody else in the kitchen getting me some bread and somebody else getting me something else and then I had another one queuing at the phone to keep my place for me. You had to walk to the phone and his cell was next to it and I used to say, 'Get me the phone tonight.' I used to give him a phone card every week for that. Then I had somebody going to the shop every week for me because it was a haul going from one end of the jail to the other carrying £25 worth of shopping. Tins of tuna, tins of beans, tins of fruit, desiccated milk, I tried all sorts. My pad had every fucking thing in it; it was like something out of *Porridge*! I even had an armchair. The only thing that was missing was my own telly.

I used to play cards with this lad – we played for a Mars bar – and I beat him every night for eight weeks on the trot and he was devastated. He used to support Liverpool and I was a Manchester United fan, so we used to have a bit of fun over the football. I recall Man U won the double; they had beaten Liverpool. I had bets on with the Scousers and I won about 20 phone cards.

There were a few times when I had to stop bullying. This Welsh lad nicknamed Taffy was about 55 and he used to make puzzles and give them to the lads, and somebody had gone in and pinched his teabags, coffee and stuff like that. I went into the television room where everyone was watching *EastEnders*, turned the lights up to command their attention and said, 'Right, listen, we are in here and it's a hard enough time for any of us, but when some fucker is pinching off people's pads I'm not having it. When I find them they will end up getting a fucking good hiding off me.'

All the lads contributed stuff and Taffy was over the moon.

A couple of young kids from Manchester, brothers, only about 21 or 22, came in and they were scared. I told them, 'Any trouble, just come and see me.'

'It's great in here because you stop all the bullying,' they said, and they loved it. I just wouldn't tolerate it. I'd tell people to behave.

There were a lot of lost souls in there. One lad had a pair of trainers sent in from his gran, who had saved up all her fucking money, and you can imagine saving up £80 or £90. I can't remember the lad's name.

I said to him, 'Where are your fucking new trainers?'

'I sold them for a bag,' he went.

He had sold his new trainers for a £2 bag of brown! He was walking around with a pair of working boots on and I said to this other guy, 'Give the lad his trainers back,' and I gave him a phone card for them and he got them back.

I met this lad called Crabby, big and intimidating-looking, six foot four and about 18 stone. He was in for pinching a police car and ramming it. As unfriendly as he seemed, he was all right when you got to know him. He used to wear these tracksuit bottoms with a pair of shorts over them.

I said, 'You look like a fucking rooster.'

He laughed his fucking head off and said, 'I've worn these for about three months and nobody has said anything until you have.'

He was building this model boat out of matchsticks and he was OK.

I remember when it started snowing and it was really bad, and out of 600 prisoners there were 150 fighting each other with snowballs, 75 or so on each side. In this prison there were what they called 'E-lines', E1 and E2, each representing a different camp of prisoners. So the two camps were fighting each other with snowballs and there were 75 snowballs coming all at once from one side and 75 from the other. I came out and walked through the middle of them, and the minute I stepped in between them not one more snowball got thrown; it was like Mother Teresa walking through a crowd.

I said, 'Anybody fucking dare and I'll bray them!'

Everyone was laughing, saying that nobody dared throw a snowball at me. And when I came back through them, I did it just to piss them off, and they were all saying, 'Here's the big fella, don't throw a snowball.'

Sometimes I would go and see Johno and I would play cards and have a bit of fun.

Then there was this fucking idiot, a flat-nosed, cauliflower-lugged rugby player, in there. He thought he could fight. This thing was on TV called *Man O Man*, where the girls had to pick a date from a group of men and every time they rejected one the girl pushed him into a swimming pool. We used to have a bet and everyone would pick one of the male contestants and we would bet a Mars bar on the winner.

I said, 'I'll tell you what the best thing is to do: we'll pick ten numbers out of the hat, and the ten of us each had a number representing our bet.'

I used to say, 'Look at the fucking clip of that one. I've got a ginger-haired one, that's me fucked with winning.'

We were all sitting watching it about teatime on a Saturday night. There were four settees and some of the lads said, 'Move along, big fella,' so I moved along. 'Move along! Move along!' they went.

'For fuck's sake!' I yelled.

When you fight, you don't even think about it, it's like, boom! I fucking shattered this rugby player's jaw with a cracking right man-stopper! I also fucking cracked his cheekbone and knocked him into the following week. One of the screws witnessed it and he grassed me up, the fucking scumbag.

Later, a screw came by and said, 'Right, you're going to get moved to Walton.'

Fucking nightmare! They sent me to Walton Jail, in Liverpool. I remember it was about nine o'clock in the morning and the whole jail got shut down and all the screws came and they were saying, 'Look, Brian, you are too big for us to be fighting with.'

Invitingly, I said, 'Come on, make your fucking pay!'

This young screw asked, 'Can I come in, big fella? I don't want any trouble, you're too big for me. Look, we don't want any fucking trouble with you, it's the rules, the fucking rules, and we can only go with what the governor fucking tells us. You can battle me all day long, but you'll only get more jail,' he sensibly said.

'Oh, fuck it!' I said. 'I'll just fucking go then.'

When I got to Walton, I thought, I'm going to have fucking trouble here, it's full of Scousers. The place was fucking huge and, in comparison, all the other jails I had been to were just baby jails. This place was packed to the rafters with 1,700 prisoners and 600 screws. With its three tall storeys, it reached up to the sky.

This screw came up to me in reception and growled, 'Name? Stand back, there!'

Don't get fucking clever, I thought. I don't care how many of you there are.

I gave him the Cockerill stare and said, 'Cockerill, blah, blah, blah.'

He said, 'Do you want a job?'

I said, 'Do fish swim?'

He said, 'Right, you'll have a job in two days because they like big lads in reception.'

What he meant was they like them to beat the nonces, the sex cases, when they came in.

I'd been in my pad a couple of days when he came in and said, 'You're at work in the morning. Clear your pad, you're going downstairs.'

When you work in reception, you have got to be in a cell on the lower landing because they come for you first thing, at six in the morning. We were sorting out things for those being discharged and for those going to court. I was working on the clothes boxes with this lad who was a bit of a moaning cunt. I was keeping myself right and I thought, I can't hit any fucker else because the screws have put me on reception. I'd been told, 'Any more of your crazy capers and you're going to Albany,' which is on the Isle of Man. It was fucking Albany or Parkhurst, on the Isle of Wight.

I met this lad called Steve Connors. He used to run about 400 nightclub doors with his mate and there was a lad who worked for him called Mark Stiles. Scousers. They were all right, they were sound, and they were on my landing as they worked in the kitchens and also had to be up early.

During association period, we had a bit of fun there. We never got to go to the gym because of our jobs, but I met this footballer called Jimmy Kelly who had been done for fighting. He showed me this circuit training and I started training with him and this other lad, and then we got some makeshift weights made out of old wholesale-size jam tubs. We would fill these tubs with water; they weren't dead heavy, maybe 20 pounds, but in sets they became heavy. I got a thick brush shank and loaded tubs on each end and had myself a 100-pound barbell to train with.

I was on reception one night when people came in from the courts and some of them were pointed out to me as nonces.

We used to throw things at the nonces, like newspaper balls, and I would scowl at them and say, 'Who are you fucking looking at?'

This bloke came in who had been done for taking a little girl, Sophie Hook, aged nine, out of a tent. He had sexually abused, battered and beaten her, tossed her into the sea and left her to die in North Wales. His name was the same as the dead billionaire Howard Hughes.

He came in on a Sunday and they said, 'It has got to be right with this cunt because if you fuck up ...'

'To the max,' I said. They all knew what it meant: take the fucking piss.

Hughes was a towering guy of about six foot eight, but he didn't have the stature to go with it; he was skinny. And he was terrified. Behind this man's face, a past of paedophiliac tendencies simmered; he was a ticking timebomb! He used to wander round his hometown of Colwyn Bay, North Wales, dragging his Rottweiler behind him, and everyone was afraid of him.

In July 1995, Sophie Hook was sleeping in a tent with her two cousins in her uncle's garden. From there she was abducted by the sex monster Hughes, who was already notorious in his neighbourhood for his paedophilia and other anti-social tendencies.

A walker found Sophie's tiny body washed up on a beach at Craig-y-Don, Llandudno, that same month.

Following his trial at Chester Crown Court in 1996, Hughes was given three life sentences, with a recommendation from the judge that he should never be released.

That is not the end of the story. Later on, it was claimed by a disgruntled ex-girlfriend of Pc David Gardner that he sold to the press, before the trial began, a police custody photograph of Hughes and confidential psychiatric reports.

I know I sometimes put policemen down, but this copper was pursued through the courts and investigated by other policemen. Not surprisingly, Pc Gardner pleaded not guilty to two charges of corruptly receiving £5,000 for selling police information and receiving extra money for the photograph between 31 July and 30 November 1995.

The copper was not arrested until five years after the alleged incident, following his break-up with his girlfriend. The woman went to the police in 2000 claiming Pc Gardner had told her he handed over the photograph to the media in return for money.

Everything was going fine for Pc Gardner until the police discovered his thumbprint on the report! He claimed it was as a result of his innocently examining the document.

After a farcical trial, Pc Gardner, from Colwyn Bay, was cleared of all charges. I know Pc Gardner was suspended from the force while an internal inquiry was carried out. I do know what happened to the poor guy, but if it makes him feel any happier, I can tell him that I gave Hughes a pair of cut-off jeans that made him look like fucking Robinson Crusoe! I also gave him a white shoe and a brown shoe, a brown sock and a black sock, and I ripped a sleeve off one of the shirts and gave him a ripped jumper. I gave him all the fucking shit.

This monster stood there draped in a mishmash of clothing and he looked like something the sea had washed up. I glared at him and spat, 'You cunt. Young little girls, fucking their lives up. What are you fucking looking at?'

The pervert cringed as he grovelled to the governor, who had just turned up, 'He's looking at me, he's going to hit me, he's going to hit me!'

I bet he didn't give little Sophie a chance to tell on him when he was raping her! One of the screws, Mr Bolt, called out, 'Come on, big fella, I would love for you to fucking chin him, but we can't, we would only make it better for the cunt.'

I shouted to Hughes, 'You fucking screamer!'

He jumped out of his fucking skin and shit himself.

When I worked in the reception kitchen, we were doing the fruit and had to crush up about 400 oranges, so we had fresh orange juice, with a little bit of water added, for a couple of weeks. Then one of the screws gave us some steaks. It was like a scene from *Goodfellas*: we were cooking steaks and drinking fresh orange, and a screw came in and said, 'Fucking hell, it's like the fucking Grand Hotel in here.'

This screw, Dicky, the SO (Senior Officer), was sound. So were all the screws on reception – sound as a pound.

One night I had the shits, though it wasn't from drinking all that fresh orange juice. The doctor said he wanted me to stay in the cell for a day. The next day I went back and he gave me some medicine, but out of the blue he said, 'What are you doing wearing tracksuit bottoms?'

He was Scottish, a daft fucking prick, fucking scumbag cunt. A right wanker, he was. Can you tell I didn't like him? If I saw him in the street now, I would knock the fucker clean out, he was that much of a scar-faced bastard.

He was, like, 'What are you looking at there, big fella?' A proper fucking worky-ticket bastard. He twisted his face and said, 'You're not wearing those bottoms in here.' A bully, a weak, spineless cunt.

I gritted my teeth and retorted, 'Here, I have to wear them because my legs are too big and I've got scars on my legs and they get irritated by the material the jeans are made from. There have been three doctors that have said categorically that I can't wear jeans.'

'You are wearing jeans in this jail!' he commanded.

I screwed my face up and eyed him up and down and blasted, 'I'm fucking not, like!'

He continued with his bombastic stance. 'You will wear them or you will be put in the block!'

I said, 'Well, do what you have to do, big man!' He looked at me with this thunderous face and I said, 'Don't get fucking clever with me. I don't give a fuck who you are!'

I got put in my pad and Dicky came round and said, 'What the fuck's happened?'

When I told him, he blasted at the doctor, 'Fuck you, you Scotch cunt. Cheeky cunt, messing with my fucking lad, he is working down there!'

The next day I walked through with my tracksuit bottoms on and nobody stopped me.

Working in reception, you were out of your cell all day, but you only had about 20 minutes at night to get to the phone and speak with your loved ones, even though you were out of your cell from six in the morning until very late at night. Time flew by with these 14- and 16-hour working days. Being locked in your cell made minutes seem like hours and hours seem like days; jail seemed to last for ever.

When I was in Haverigg, I was starting to put weight on and reached 22 stone, but now, without training and regular piles of the right food, I had dropped down to under 19 stone.

This lad called Duckdale came in, a big fat, farmer type, about

25 stone and six foot four, but only about 22. He was very reminiscent of Lee Duffy, but bigger!

He was staring at me and I barked, 'Who are you fucking looking at?'

I could tell he wasn't scared of me. He'd got 10 years for glassing a copper and taking his eye out and 12 years for armed robbery – 22 years in total! He didn't give a fuck about anyone and was spewing up all over when he tasted the food. 'You can shove it up your arse,' he mumbled.

His stinking spew was everywhere and we had to clean this fucking rubbish up. Well, I didn't, but the other lads in reception did.

When this Duckdale character was getting his gear, two screws went off and left us to it. Three of the reception lads were tooled up and quietly followed Duckdale into the shower area. I was having none of it, as I hated bullying. I thought, Fuck this, they're going to kill the cunt! I went into the shower area to make sure he wasn't being set about.

Out he came with a towel wrapped around him. And then the cunt ran at me!

I slipped his punch, banged two sharp blows to the ribcage and his bowels went. He hit the floor like a bag of shit, literally – he shit himself!

Everyone knew we were going to hit the cunt, everybody wanted him battered. Anyway, I took him out with two lightning shots. Boom! Boom!

They went, 'Fucking hell, one minute he was there and the next minute he was on the fucking floor. Big fella, that was brilliant, fucking brilliant.'

I'd gone back into the shower area to make sure he was all right, because three on to one is not my game, but I'd ended up dropping the cunt. After that, they were all calling him 'shitty arse'. The gardening lads gathered some acorns, cut them up and put them in a bag and said to Duckdale, 'Here, shitty arse, here are your droppings.'

To be fair to Duckdale, your bowels can go with a body shot. But they continued torturing him with humiliating tactics and his fucking face was bright red. He wasn't the big man any more.

Afterwards I said, 'Do you want another go?'

He was, like, 'No, no!'

I'd brayed the cunt and I was king of the fucking jail.

A week later, he got shipped out to Frankland Prison in Durham.

Dicky put a good word in for me to get me to a real cushy jail, in Wetherby, North Yorkshire. We got to Thorpe Arch Prison and I was expecting to be transferred to Rudgate, a category-D open prison next door to Thorpe Arch.

But the screw on reception said, 'You're in cat C, you. You're not a D, you're staying here.'

I remember Dicky saying, 'Any problems when you get there, tell them to phone me.'

I said, 'I was told by the officer that I was a cat D.'

He backtracked and said, 'I have got it here, and you are a cat D, you're not cat C.'

They were trying to get one over on me and wanted to put me in this cat-C prison instead of Rudgate, which had just had a change of name and become Wealstun Prison.

To cut a long story short, they put me in Wealstun but warned, 'Any carry-on and you'll be straight back in here.'

You could freely walk about anywhere you wanted! You could go and watch telly, play snooker. Wealstun really was like being in a fucking holiday camp. When I looked back to the other prisons I had been in, I cringed!

The novelty soon wore off, though, because you had too much time on your hands. When I was working on the clothes boxes in Walton, the time flew by.

I'd been in Wealstun for about four weeks when this lad fucked off over the fence. Some just couldn't handle the time they had on their hands or the drastic change from a mainstream prison.

This place had more booze in it than a park full of teenagers on a Friday night! One time I was pissed and I was, like, 'I'm going home, me. I'm going home.' The next day I had a hangover like a mushroom cloud. My head felt like a nail gun had zapped it! I must have had just three or four tins, but I hadn't had a drink for about six, seven, eight months.

In there, I got to meet Kev Richardson and he was, like, 'All right, son.' He put his arms around me because I hadn't seen him for fucking years and said, 'Fucking hell, you big cunt, you are massive.'

And I was still big, even though I had lost three or four stone. Kev had looked after me when I was a kid, and now we started training together in the gym.

15 THE FIGHTING COCKERILL

BEFORE I WENT to jail, I used to see a lot of Ernie Bewick and he came to see me now and then at Wealstun. Ernie has been called a gangland killer and an enforcer. He is neither of those, but I can tell you he is one of the nicest men I have come across.

For those of you who might not have heard of Ernie Bewick, I'll fill you in on the details. It was 7 December 1997 when convicted drug dealer Tony Waters died outside the Eastender pub in High Street East, Sunderland. In an incident that stemmed from the night before, Waters went looking for Ernie with the intention of doing him some damage over an incident between Ernie and two other men in Luciano's restaurant in the town.

I would never underestimate a man like Ernie. He was fully aware that Waters was a drug dealer and that he himself could make the difference between Sunderland being awash with drugs or staying relatively drug free. And, so long as he was in charge of the doors of certain pubs and clubs, he would keep drugs out.

Viv Graham enforced the same standards in Newcastle when he was alive. Like Ernie, he disapproved of drugs. And, just as some people wanted Viv out of the way so that they could sell drugs on his patch on Tyneside, other dealers were hoping to gain a free hand in Ernie's territory, on Wearside.

It was Tony Waters's ambition to deal drugs in Sunderland that brought his life to an untimely end.

The whole thing got of hand and exploded like a can of worms mixed with gunpowder! Word was spreading around town that it had taken seven of them to sort out Scott Waters, a rumour apparently started by Scott himself. People were looking to Ernie to see what he would do to scotch this rumour. It looked like he was being sucked into a web of lies and deceit and he reacted in a way that was out of character.

Facing the very same crowd that had told him about the rumours Scott Waters was spreading, Ernie couldn't back down, so he confronted him head on and ended up knocking him out.

People were walking about with guns looking for Ernie Bewick. They were looking in all the wrong places, it would seem, which suggests that they probably wanted word to get back to him that they were looking for him about the previous night's fight. They wanted to send a message of strength and also to frighten Ernie into staying away so that they could sell their drugs. Certain people were advised to stay away from the town centre because there was 'going to be trouble'.

Ernie being Ernie, he wasn't going to stay away, because it was his territory and he had to show others that he wasn't a man to hide away over something like this.

On entering the Eastender pub, Ernie saw Tony and they acknowledged each other. The story goes that Tony asked what had happened the night before and in his understated fashion Ernie told the truth. Tony was having none of it and issued an insult that was designed to cause further trouble: he called Ernie a 'liar'.

Scott Waters was not a fighter and it would go against a man like Ernie's code of conduct to hand out the thrashing Scott said he had received, but it didn't pull any weight with Tony. Ernie was told to get outside the door, clearly for a one-to-one, but as Ernie walked towards the door a bottle crashed off his head. Ernie then approached the man who had thrown the bottle, Tony's stepson, but the man's mother got in between her son and Ernie and became protective towards her cherub of a son.

The altercation seemed to have settled and one of the doormen, Ritchie Laws, took over the task of calming everyone down, but Tony's stepson had a liking for throwing bottles and threw another one. It hit Ernie square in the face, but he didn't retaliate.

He pleaded with Tony to forget it, but Tony would not let it go and was starting to make a show in front of people. He was shouting that Ernie was going to be shot, and the argument continued as they went down the stairs. Tony poked his finger into Ernie's face and still Ernie did not retaliate.

Outside the pub, Tony Waters met his death in a fight that was ferocious by any man's standards.

Ernie called me on the night he killed Tony Waters and said, 'Look, Brian, what shall I do?'

I said, 'You can come and stay down my house.'

I felt sorry for him, as he had been pushed into it. He was just a fighter. He didn't do drugs; he was just a proper fighter on the door.

I used to go and see him and have a drink. I would often be up there in Sunderland on a weekend and feel safe when he took us round the tough west end of the town. He wouldn't back down to anyone.

I used to go and help him in case he needed me. We used to run about together and people would say about him, 'Look at that monster, there, fucking bastard.' At one pub, where there were five or six doormen, I said to them, 'Do you want a fucking go or what? If you want a fucking go, I'll wipe you out here.' Then I told them, 'If you want to fucking stare at me like that again on the way out, then book yourself a trip to hospital!'

They all shit themselves.

Going back to when I was in jail, Ernie came to see me and the other faces were saying, 'Oh, you come to see him, you don't come to see us.'

Ernie said, 'They're all going mad with me here because I never went to see them.'

Stevie Hammer, another really nice lad I met in there, had a lot of respect for Ernie, and so did many others.

I met a lad called Mark Steele who'd got nine years for shooting a doorman and hitting a girl. He used to put the pads on and when I let rip he'd say, 'Fucking hell, Brian, you're punching my fucking hands off!'

One of the lads used to sneak the pads in at night over the fence. I had a pair of mitts that I used for hitting the fucking pads. People would come and watch me, 10 or 15 lads sitting in the dorm watching me do the pads of an evening.

I would do three three-minute rounds three or four nights each week and it was a bit of fun. I met a lot of people in there. Geoff Brown, he was sound. Johnny the Pirate, he was all right with me. There were also a load of rats – ex-coppers and bent solicitors – and they were all category D because they were classed as white-collar criminals.

After you were there for a while, you got 'town visits'. You were allowed to go home for something like ten hours on the weekend, and every second weekend you could go home and see your girlfriend and have a few drinks or whatever.

I'd been in Wealstun for about six weeks when I got a job doing paperwork, stamping things and all that shit. They said there was a job coming up in the outside swimming baths, which meant you could work outside the prison. I had an advantage because I had a first-aid certificate and I had done the swimming course, so I got the job. I worked at one of the sports centres, just sweeping and mopping the floors, but at least I was out. One bloke was the manager of the centre and the other one was a bit of a tit, giving me all his shitty jobs. It was, 'Make me some tea,' and the likes.

I could go on the sun beds and in the pool, and I was allowed to wear my own tracksuits, so I felt just like a normal person. I know it sounds nothing, but, when you are in jail, it is a lot. I was assisting this lass helping handicapped kids learn to swim. This was enjoyable and rewarding because you see them trying like mad to swim and you are teaching them and helping them.

There was a lad called Billy at the sports centre and I was helping him with his boxing. They didn't know there who I was, that I was the top fighter and all that. They thought that I was just some lunatic from the North-East, taxing drug dealers, nicked for shootings and murders and all these mad fucking charges. I didn't tell lies, because they get the paperwork to say what you are in for.

On a Sunday, somebody would nip up from Teesside and drop me some money off at the place, and Billy would keep it for me. I used this to buy cakes and other luxuries. I started training and doing a few jobs that were coming in. I was putting a bit of weight on: I got to about 19 ½ stone.

We had a tug-of-war competition. One of the lads was a body-builder type, about 14 stone, a really strong lad. Another was a footballer. Johnny was about 14 stone. Several of them were about 13, 14 stone, and strong. Stevie Hammer was about 17 stone, Geoff Brown about 15 stone and this other big fat lad was 16 stone; all big, heavy lads.

I could do an hour's circuit training and Stevie said, 'For fuck's sake, you've been doing that for an hour non-stop!'

These were all big lads, but they never had timing, just as Lee

Duffy never had it, and that is why I knew he couldn't beat me. I've got stringy arms and movement, and you just go boom, boom, boom! It is the fast punches that knock you out, not the big slow ones.

There were about ten men in each tug-of-war team and I said to my boys, 'Listen, lads, team talk. These will probably beat us on the first one, but it's the first one to three. They won't fucking last three pulls. So listen to me.'

Being the biggest and heaviest on our team, I went on the anchor end of the rope. All the lads were in studded football boots because we were on mud. I ordered, 'Breathe fucking in.'

Regrettably, there were some big fat fuckers on the opposing team, each of the fat cunts weighing about 18, 19 stone.

'Hold them, hold them,' I shouted.

I was pulling and the other team were laughing and saying, 'All right, big fella, have you got any weight on your team?'

At that stage, they were beating us 1–0, but in the end we fucking hammered them 3–1. After the second pull, they were fucking purple in the face, because we were holding for about a minute or two minutes.

The second pull we held for about a minute, and they were still laughing. After three minutes I roared, 'Pull, pull,' and we dragged them all over the field and they were falling over.

They were bringing on other people and I said, 'You can't have him. This big fat one went purple and nearly had a fucking heart attack.'

I seemed to be spending more time outside jail than inside. I remember once when I went home and my mate Chino had some trouble with these two lads who had taken 15 grand off him and wouldn't pay him back. The two of us fucking chased them. They didn't know I was in the car; they thought I was still in jail. I jumped out and could see them grimace as I said, 'Where's that fucking money?'

They fucking shit themselves, and the next day they paid Chino the 15 grand. I looked after him and he would come and pick me up and give me 50 quid every other week.

I got out of jail four days early, as I'd been in police custody for that amount of time. Mum and Dad picked me up and we were driving along and I thought, Thank fuck for that.

I had done it. It's nothing to some people, but I hadn't really done jail before, so it meant a lot to me. I got home and thought it was great that you could just go to the toilet when you wanted to. I know I finished my time in open conditions and had some freedom, but the earlier parts of my sentence had stuck with me. Now I could go to the fridge and get a nice, cold glass of milk, use proper toilet roll, watch telly when I wanted, have a beer when I fancied one and pop out in the car.

I'd got a four-year driving ban as well, and I had to resit my driving test. But, even before retaking it, I was allowed to drive a car with a provisional licence, but with learner plates on and as long as I had a full licence holder with me.

I was fucking out, and people were saying, 'He won't be able to fight,' and all this shite.

I weighed about 19 ½ stone, but I'd been about 22 ½ when I went in, so I had lost three stone and I was fucking fit as fuck, and I mean superfit. I would say I was the fittest I have ever been in my life. I jumped up to around 21 ½ stone in three months. I was fucking huge, as big as a shed.

I was planning to go in for the Strongest Man in Britain and I was squatting phenomenal weights, 600 pounds for 20 reps. I was going in for that and a few other world records, all for charity, to help kids in need and causes like that.

It was my mate's birthday and I hadn't been out for ages, so I went out and had a few drinks in the Steampacket, in Middlesbrough, which was a rave club but is shut down now.

I had had my night out after being imprisoned and I was ready for war. The rat-catcher was back. Now where were the fucking rats?

I had a fight with this lad called John Metz. It started when he said, 'You won't be as good a fighter now,' and he was going on all fucking night like that.

Anyway, he hit me with a bottle in the face, so I became a raging bull and fucking battered him all over and broke his jaw. I nearly flatlined the cunt. I think I fractured his skull as well. As usual, the police were involved and it got dropped. Metz fucked off in the end and nothing happened.

Mind, he came back and I said, 'Come on then, let's go head-to-head!' but he didn't want to fucking know; it was all sorted.

Metz was about 14 stone and, in his heyday, he'd had about 160 amateur fights. I wouldn't say he was an idiot; he was probably one of the top ten fighters in Middlesbrough. Yet he still hit me with a bottle!

Anyway, when I bashed Metz, I hit him repeatedly on the floor and I picked him up and rammed him through the ceiling. You can't take chances with people like that, especially since he was a boxer. You've got to destroy them. Once you have got hold of them, be sure you don't make the mistake I made with Garside when I let him get back up. Make sure you fucking destroy them.

The Steampacket was so rough that you would cut yourself just going in there. Everybody was going, 'All right, big fella?' and jumping about, happy. Thomo came in, and you can always tell when he has had a fight. He'd had one with David Allison, Allo, the lad who killed Lee Duffy.

Allo was sitting with a load of lads. I had never met him, I had only seen him in jail years ago, and that was for all of ten seconds. I turned round and he was sitting there showing these photos to his companions. Dave Woody and Kenny Woodier were sitting near him; they were both all right with me. I was sitting with Pecker and a few other lads. There were about 20 people in there in all.

Thomo said, 'All right, big fella,' because he had been out with the Honeyman brothers, Dene and millionaire club owner Norman. His racehorse had won 80 grand for him, so he was out all weekend paying for the lads' booze.

It ended up with Thomo fighting, and Thomo fell down because he had been out all weekend and was pissed. Then, for no reason, Allo started hitting him with a stool and Thomo said, 'Brian, help me!'

I couldn't leave him, so I said to Jamie Broderick, who was with Allo and this other big one, 'Look, break it up.'

I had this big thick gold chain on and Allo grabbed it and tried to bite my nose. I pulled him off like removing a maggot from a bone and gave him head-to-head combat – about 15 face-crushing headbutts to his dial. This wild head ride smashed his face to a pulp and he was half-unconscious, lying there like a splintered statue with everyone looking on.

There were about half a dozen good Samaritans trying to pull me off him. Kenny's brother was hanging on to my arm and as I was smacking Allo, he was going up and down. None of them could get me off Allo; I was attached to him like a barnacle. I picked him up and with a thinly veiled scowl I growled at the wannabe hard man, 'Let's fight outside and then we can fight properly!'

When I got him outside … bang, bang, bang! The body shots were not meant to floor him; they were designed to inflict pain. In the end, I gangster-slapped him with my shovel-sized hand and he went down like a squashed tomato!

I went, 'What are you doing down there? Look at me,' and I started doing a sort of Red Indian rain dance and was fucking about.

His mates were saying to him, 'Look at the fucking state of you, battered to a pulp!'

I will be honest here. I didn't know it was Allo, the guy that killed Duffy. I asked the lads who he was and they said, 'It's Allo.'

'The one that did Lee Duffy?'

'Yes.'

It would be nice to think that I got him back in a way for Lee, because of what he had done.

So, after finding that out, I said to Allo, 'Here, come here, there's a kick up the fucking arse from a man to a little boy.' Then I asked, 'Where's your fucking mate, Joe Livo?' Joe was one of the top fighters.

Worry lines came across people's faces as I rolled my eyes and said, 'You're fucking shite! Come on then, I'll tell you what I'll do, I'll give you a fucking chance. I'll fight you and Joe together.'

Joe lived nearby. Stamping about with rage, I said, 'I'll fight you in the field over the road from his fucking house. I'll fucking batter the both of you, you brainless morons.'

I was nearly 22 stone. I was still training on the boxing pads two or three times a week, doing circuits twice a week and a five-minute circuit every morning. I was working out like a demented demon. I was on the bag doing four three-minute rounds once a week, a ten-minute round on a Wednesday, and on Monday, Wednesday and Friday I would do six twos.

After I beat Allo and others like him, people were paying me again for looking after them and I also did a few taxes. But the real action was with now the fag men. These cigarette dealers were going to shoot my mate, one of the gypsy lads at the caravan site. They asked me, 'Will you have a word with them and we'll give you a wedge?'

I replied, 'I want two and a half grand off each of you.'

There were four of them, so they gave me ten grand to stop

this trouble. And then Buster brought a lad whose son was going to get shot by these Hartlepool lads.

His jaw dropped when I said, 'Give me two grand.'

Wide-eyed, he exclaimed, 'Two fucking grand?'

In a nanosecond, I had transformed from an affable giant to a scowling demon: 'Here, fuck off out of my house, it doesn't matter, two grand! How much do you think it would cost? So you don't value your son's life at two grand. That's a week's wages to you and you're whinging about two poxy grand! If you want it sorted, I'm upping it to three grand now!'

I got my wage and I said, 'Fuck off,' and threw him out.

About two days later I found out that the lads weren't even going to shoot him, but I still spoke on the phone to the lad, who was in hiding, and I said, 'You are going to get shot, you, you cunt.'

I had to build him up to the fact that he was going to get shot and then smooth it away for him after that.

I would command £500 off people who had trouble off someone. They would tell me, 'He's going to fill me in.'

I would say, 'Give me a grand and I'll go and sort it out.'

Half the time I was making money for old rope. But these things were sorted simply because of my involvement, and my reputation preceded me. They are not paying for Mrs Jones's son next door, who they don't know from Adam. It is me they want.

Getting back to Allo, when I had offered him and Joe Livo out, this lass said, 'Joe doesn't want to fight with you.'

I said, 'What's that? Joe doesn't want to what?' and I quipped, 'Joe can't fucking fight me!'

I had this £600 suit made by a tailor called Joe Hind in Newcastle and I wore it to see Ernie Bewick in Sunderland. Ernie, who is always in a tracksuit, took the piss and chuckled, 'Fucking hell, you look like something out of *The Blues Brothers*.'

While I was up there, Ernie had some trouble in this nightclub called the Office. Kev Whitehead and a lad who was a former British judo champion had been in and they had stabbed another lad. After running about, I got Whitehead's mate and said, 'Get that fucking Whitehead on the blower.'

Eventually I spoke to Whitehead on the phone and seethed, 'Come and fight me now! You think you're the best fucking fighter in Sunderland. Prove it!'

His arse had gone and he was telling people, 'I don't want to fight Brian. It was that fucking Thomo who was causing the trouble.'

I went back and Ernie was over the moon. I'm not saying that Ernie couldn't fight, because he could. It was me that warned him, 'You'll get into trouble with this cunt. I'll sort it out.'

Anyway, to cut to the chase, after all this fucking carry-on I went to Blazes nightclub in Middlesbrough, where they used to give me a few quid for helping out. I was standing with this new suit on and a lad came up to me and said, 'Who are you fucking looking at?'

I looked him in the eye and I was stunned! It was Mickey Salter but he didn't recognise me. He was Paul Salter's brother and they were both top fighters.

I squinted and said, 'Watch this!'

'Watch wha…?'

I nutted him and fucking hit him with a clubbing right hand, and Kev Hower – he is dead now, as well as Mickey Salter, God rest their souls – came over. I was lacing into Salter and working away at his face, giving him the bare-knuckle ride with the speed of a one-armed paperhanger. I hit him repeatedly in the head and smashed his cheekbone with such force that it split! The bone went through his nose and right into his head and nearly killed him. A few years later, he got stabbed to death in the face.

Kev commented, 'Friggin' hell, Brian, that wasn't a fight, that was annihilation. I've never seen anything like it. That was just unbelievable.'

Bear in mind, Mickey was a top fighter. Even so, he was destroyed within five seconds. After he had been glued and pinned back together, he went to the Bongo club with his brother Paul, a boxer, who said, 'Who the fuck has done that to you?'

'Brian Cockerill!' Mickey told him.

A couple of years ago, these gypsy friends of mine were on the receiving end of trouble from this National Front bully, a big fucking skinhead. I had been out all weekend doing what you do, it was the Monday afternoon and I was fucked, so I thought, If I don't go down there and sort it out, I will feel a shithouse.

I'd had a tough weekend and I wasn't at my best. The SAS do tests and get to the other side, and then they do 20-mile walks. I don't do that, but I do other things to programme my mind, to get myself ready to fight.

I went down there and there were about 30 gypsies and 20 or 30 of the skinhead's lads. They were all standing with their baseball bats and their machetes, fucking all sorts, with a chilling menace about them. It reminded me of the 'house of horrors' attack; it was like going to the slaughter.

As I jumped over the wall to get to them I nearly fell over it. I made a right cunt of myself!

I grabbed the lad and his mate and said, 'Nobody goes in people's houses.'

I picked up the first lad, rammed him into the wall and threw him. I hit the other lad with a body shot and he crumpled like a sheet of paper. But then he came back at me! I hit him with another body shot and he tried to poke my eye out, so I bit his ear clean off. I bit all the way through the bone and the gristle, chewed it off and spat it into the road. I should have spat it down the drain; he had been bullying old people and kids.

The one I'd tried to demolish the wall with, I battered him to a pulp. I must have hit him about 15 times in the face and broke just about every bone in his face! Let's put it this way, he wouldn't be able to play the flute any more. His teeth were smashed so bad that he looked like he was spitting feathers. His face was a fucking mess, and he was supposed to be the best fighter in that area.

After it was over, this lad said, 'I'm cock-a-hoop that you've beaten him because he's a fucking bully.'

Once when I was in a club this lad came up to me – he was about 19 stone and six foot two – and said, 'I'm the best fighter in Guisborough.'

I gave him the Cockerill stare and replied, 'No, you're not!'

He stopped in his tracks and asked, 'Well, who is then?'

I'm sure I don't need to tell you what came next!

When he heaved his blood-spattered body up off the floor he mumbled, 'I'm your mate.'

I nutted him again and said, 'I haven't even fucking punched you yet and I've dropped you twice, and guess what? *I* am the best fighter in fucking Guisborough!'

16 MURDERS, KIDNAPPINGS AND ASSAULTS

MY WIFE, AMANDA, looks after me brilliantly. She does all my food, she looks after everyone who comes to the house and she doesn't go out drinking. She pushes me and keeps me right. Years ago, I didn't give a fuck about anybody, I would be in trouble all the time, but since I met Amanda I have never been in trouble, other than once for driving a car with no 'L' plates!

Not long ago I was pulled in during a murder inquiry. If they were going to get me for a murder, they would have smashed my door in with the armed squad but, to save the front door from getting clattered, I handed myself in. They questioned me over the Darren Manders murder and said, 'We know you've done it.'

They were just fishing.

'If I'd done it you wouldn't be telling me how I had done it,' I said.

The guy was murdered somewhere in Middlesbrough; he had been lifted over a fence or something into a wooded area. I think he was hit with a baseball bat. Obviously, I got let out for that. I have been fucking blamed for a good few murders and once they came for me after a man was shot dead in Leicester because I had worked on the door for him. I am still their biggest target and I will always be target number one in that area, but there will be other, newer targets.

They are still trying to get me for murders, kidnappings, assaults and the amount of people who have had broken arms, legs and fucking things.

A few people have said to the police, 'You'd have to be Inspector Clouseau to catch him. He's too smart for you.'

Back in 1994, I worked in a pub called Birches, a brutal place, fucking rough, a bit like the Top Hat in Spennymoor. In the first few weeks, I must have knocked out about 15 people, daft cunts causing trouble. About 400 people used to go in on a Monday, but after about two months, with me being there, there were only 200 people going in. It was all women coming in now, all the wankers had gone – all the wrecking-crew type of people.

One New Year, there were about 25 or 30 troublemakers in there. I walked in and asked, 'Have any of you got anything to say?'

Not one of them would have said boo to a goose, because they knew that, no matter what they did that night, even if they beat me, I would be back. I was well known for searching people out with unremitting cruelty!

I was in the Birches talking to brothers Terry and Les Nivens, who worked at another pub, and they said they had problems too. I got up to go there with them and half the fucking pub came with me. The bullies at this other pub had grins on them a mile wide; they were like kids on a night out. But they soon ran off when I went in to get them. The rumour was that I had pulled out a handgun, put it to one lad's head and pulled the trigger, but it was supposed to have jammed.

Peter Fox, an ex-police inspector, owned the pub. He phoned

the police and the whole area was surrounded by armed police. Four hundred people were in there on this night – it was New Year, a Saturday night. Of the 400 people the police interviewed, all 400 said they did not see anything because they were in the toilets! They must have had some fucking big toilets in that pub.

The police said, 'We've found something, but we haven't found the gun,' so I was nicked again.

At the police station, all my clothes were taken off for the paraffin swab test for cordite. But nothing came back because it was all fucking bullshit.

Another time I went to a nightclub and the doorman refused to let me in and I was supposed to have sent someone back to smash all the windows. The police thought a shotgun was used in that attack, so they came and nicked me.

Two days later, they said they had found something and charged me again for firearms. I was held for 24 hours and then they let me go again. They were just taking the piss; they would try anything.

At one time, I had a car that could do 180 mph and the police used to chase me but they could never catch me. There were some cockney-looking lads in Hartlepool who were carrying guns in their car and the coppers were about to pull them over. But I beeped the law so they would come on to me, and they chased me, but I soon burned rubber and fucked off out of sight.

I dumped the car, ran off and hid behind a fence. The copper got out of his car and started to look around. It was about four o'clock in the morning and it was fucking raining cats and dogs. At this stage, I weighed 23 stone and I was out of breath because I had been running. Lying behind the fence, I was breathing heavily and that gave the game away – not that I was worried. 'I can see you behind that fence, you know, Brian,' the copper said.

I drew a breath and said, 'Fuck off or I'll knock you out.

What do you think it is, a game of fucking hide and seek, you black cunt?'

He ran like his arse was on fire, he was gone like a big shithouse.

I wasn't taxing as much now. People were becoming wise to the Tax Man and a lot of things had changed. The bigger dealerships had dissolved into myriads of smaller dealerships. The pickings were not as rewarding, and the less money, the less the buzz.

Taxi drivers, shop owners and others were paying me a legitimate wage and I set the wheels in motion to start up my own security company. Cockerill Securities is run legally and properly, with everything going through the books.

That is exactly what Viv Graham of Newcastle wanted to do, but then he was murdered. He never actually did it because he didn't have that chance. Anyway, I think he was more interested in gambling and spending time at other places. And, as for Lee Duffy, he was more interested in becoming the best fighter. But, if you keep punching people for nothing, you cannot expect to reach 40.

I am saying Viv was probably the best up there in Newcastle, but outside that area it would have been hard for him to make his mark. OK, he could have brought a few oxen down, but there's more to it than just brute force.

I have changed my ways from the days when I would have a drink. Then I would have a Coke and it was fucking full of Bacardi. I fucking hated it really, three-quarters Bacardi and a little bit of Coke out of a tin; it nearly took your lips off. I was just a greedy cunt and because I was so thirsty I would drink it, thinking it was all Coke. But then you would make a fool of yourself on the dance floor because of the drink, and they would laugh.

I used to scream at them, 'I'll fucking smash your face in in a minute.'

I would go fucking mad and pull a mad face and that would be enough to scare about nine out of ten of them.

I would say to people over the phone, 'If I come round there, you'd better fucking behave.' Just screaming at them down the phone would scare them. 'You know who I am, don't you?'

'Oh, yes.'

And it was done.

But now, because people know me and know my potential, I just need to speak to them in a friendly tone. It is no good saying, 'Look, give him it or I'll smash your fucking face in.' There's no good doing that because then you have got the police to worry about.

You go into a place and say, 'Look, mate, do me a favour. I will clear the job with you. You owe the man ten grand, give me five, keep five and just don't pay them the money.'

I then say to the man who is owed the money, 'I can't get it.'

I did that the other day with a lad who owed 13 grand. I said, 'You give me seven and you keep the rest.'

So I was happy and he was happy.

I knock on the door and I say, 'Look, I haven't come to cause trouble at your house, son. I wouldn't cause trouble but this outstanding needs to be paid.'

There's nothing criminal about asking someone to repay a debt, so long as you do not demand it with menaces. Mind you, some would say I could be considered a menace just from the look of me!

You don't fuck about with drugs and selling them. You can go to jail for that. But now you can go to bed and get up again and think, Thank fuck. Before, it was a nightmare of a routine. I was having to run about like a fucking lunatic.

I have done with all the lunatic stuff. I mean, like when I went to a place a few years ago to have a fight with some kids. Chaucy and some other lads came with me and these kids all came out with fucking guns and started shooting at me. It was like the St Valentine's Day Massacre – except they didn't kill me or anyone else!

The late Harry Lancaster, God rest his soul, had made the guns and sold them to these lunatics. They were all standing in front of me. It was like in *Pulp Fiction* when they all come out and start shooting. I turned around and the fucking car windows were out and the cars were riddled with bullets.

Afterwards, the lads told their mates, 'Brian fucked off. They fucking shit themselves.'

I said, 'Too fucking right we did.'

There were eight or nine people with handguns shooting at us and we were standing there with fuck all. I just had a bat in my hand that I'd got from the car. At first, I thought they were firing blanks, then I saw the windows being shot out and I thought, Fuck this, and made a sharp exit. Would you believe it, there were about 11 of us in and on a Cosworth! How no one was killed or injured, I don't know!

But the same people, I got a lot of them back. What I am saying is some things you can blag and some things you can't, but, when someone is shooting guns at you with masks on, you really can't blag that, can you? When someone comes ballied up [wearing a balaclava] with guns blazing, then you know you are in trouble.

When someone pulls a gun on you, you don't go, 'Come on then.' If they are a good shot, you are dead. If someone has got a gun, you can't outrun a speeding bullet, so there is no point in trying. It is like people with knives: I have fought people with knives who were trying to stab me, and people using bars or throwing glasses. You have got to keep trying, haven't you?

For 20 years I have been doing things, for 20 years I have been getting locked up, for 20 years I have been getting shot at and for 20 years I have had the fucking police bugging my phones, bugging my house and bugging my car.

Well, if I don't convert to security work, I'll be looking at the police for 20 more years, trying to set me up and doing this and doing that, but I have got away with it every time and it is only through my own skill and my own brain and my solicitor, Craig Beer. They have got me off so many times and they are very intelligent people.

Craig said to me, 'Brian, you have made me some money over the years. You're the best client I have ever had.'

I am not joking, and he would tell you the same himself: every night I would get phone calls asking me to sort something out or I would ring his home number because I'd been locked up again. I would leave it until six, seven, eight in the morning, though, because I didn't want to wake him and his wife up at three o'clock in the morning. I used to say, 'Just leave me in the cells until the morning.'

If they charge you for attempted murder, you know you are going to fucking court the next day, so you might as well wait and see your solicitor in court. You are not going to get bail at the police station. People panic when they get locked up, but I know if I get a solicitor I might get my bail. I must have been arrested, and I am not kidding you, about 200 times. I reckon I have been charged more than 50 times and got off.

My London connections are people I knew through others that used to live down there. They were a big firm but I'm not going to say their names.

One time I stayed in London for the weekend and went with Steve Lancaster, Robbie Armstrong and another lad to the Three Keys to see a lad called Steve Newman. We stayed at his flat and we went out to a pub called the Lilliput, where there were some big doormen.

I was wearing a tracksuit and I said, 'Am I all right for getting in or fucking what?'

'Yes, we're letting you in,' they said.

In the pub, I was shadowboxing and the legendary, former Richardson gang boss, Charlie Richardson, said, 'Bleedin' 'eck, you're a big geezer. Do me a favour, big fella – you're making everyone paranoid to death in here.'

When that pub finished serving, it all seemed to shut down! I thought, Fucking hell, we've got blues clubs, rave clubs and everything, and we go to London, the capital, and there is nothing fucking happening. Come two o'clock in the morning and everything was closed. This was not so long ago: 1993.

Eventually we found a place that was open all night, but it was a quiet place, a Turkish or Greek bar. I was jumping about and there was only one girl in the fucking place and I thought, This is fucking shit. I went to the toilet and I thought there was going to be trouble. The Turks or Greeks went home and brought guns backs because I was in there jumping about like a lunatic and they were fucking shitting themselves.

The nightclubs we went to in London had some security, but they invited me to stay and do some work for them.

I said, 'My car's being sorted, I've got to get back home.'

I had only gone down there because the armed police were looking for me after Bam Bam had threatened John the Brick.

Down there it was all right, but it wasn't my cup of tea. Mind, don't think there was loads of violence in London; there was more of that going on here, in Teesside, than down the smoke. They still fucking kill them, but they do it a lot quieter down there.

17 TO PROTECT AND SERVE

ABOUT TWO YEARS ago I got a phone call in Middlesbrough and a lady asked, 'Are you Brian Cockerill?'

I said, 'Yes, speaking.'

She said, 'Well, maybe you could help me. I have got a son, he is only 15, and he's been hooked on crack cocaine. He's been buying it off these black lads in Middlesbrough.'

Apparently, they had come down from London and opened a crack house and had been selling it to this kid. I went to see him to try to get him to come to the gym and try to get off the stuff.

I went round to the crack house and took him with me. These black lads were standing at the door and they had this doorman there to take care of any trouble. He was a big man, 18 stone and six foot three, about the same height as me.

Pointing to the lad, I said, 'If he comes to the house, I don't want you to sell anything to him.'

Recklessly, he said, 'We'll do what we want, because we're taking over this town!'

'Is that a fucking fact, now?' I said.

I told him who I was and the procedure and blah, blah, blah. He tried to pull a blade out of his pocket. He might have looked the part, but he was no match for me when I reacted instinctively. I caught him with a peach of a left hook. He was lying there unconscious on the floor and I wiped my feet on his face as I stepped over him to kick the door off its hinges!

I had lost my temper now and I could hear the rest of them inside the house scurrying like rodents to get out of the back. I was running about the house, braying anyone I could get my hands on with a vengeance.

This doorman was on the floor making gurgling sounds … he was choking. By this time, I had composed myself and realised the gravity of what my raw temper could do. He's going to fucking die here, I thought.

I didn't realise that what they do is put the crack in their mouth, wrapped in clingfilm, so that when the police pull them they can just swallow it. He was choking on a wrap of crack! I prised his lower jaw open with the toe of my trainer and asked one of the lads to reach in and clear his airway. I wasn't going to put my hand near his teeth, as the only thing with teeth that doesn't bite is a comb.

Would you believe it, this other lad pocketed the wrap he'd just taken from the monster's mouth. He was still knocked out, so they carted him off into the house where he remained out cold for nearly two hours. I only know that because I kept phoning to see if had come round, as I had pangs of guilt.

I covered my arse by saying they should get an ambulance for him. But, when he did eventually come round, he made his own way to hospital, with his jaw broken.

Another phone call, about two years ago, was from a friend of mine, Brendon, and he said, 'My sister lives in Pelham Street in Middlesbrough. She's living there and is on single-parent benefit. These lads who live in this nearby house are partying every night, and they are only young kids, maybe 22, 23, 24, and they are all on ecstasy and heroin.'

He went on to say, 'They are mentally torturing people, graffiti on the walls and things like that. They've been to the police, but they can't do anything because, every time they've been, there is no proof.'

Local people had phoned their MP in an attempt to have the problem sorted. As a last resort, they had even phoned the *Gazette* newspaper. All in all, things were still just as bad.

I arrived at the street at about six o'clock in the evening, when it was already dark, and there was a congregation of about six to eight people on one side and about five or six on the other. On seeing me, they formed one group and someone asked, 'Are you the lad that's supposed to come and help us?'

I told them I was.

Among the group there was an old woman, who said, 'I'm 84 and my husband is 80 and we've lived here for 50 years and we just can't bear it any longer.'

The old dear started crying and I said, 'Calm down, you're going to be all right. What's happened?'

She explained, 'They've written all over my windows in blood, they must have cut their hands on something and written all over the windows. They've been putting something through my letterbox. We can't sleep at night because what they are doing is they're in the loft, in the roof. They're getting on to the rooftops, lifting the tiles and shining torches into people's houses. We've phoned the police and the police have just said that they can't do anything!'

'Leave it with me,' I said.

I knocked on the door of the house where the trouble was coming from, but there was no one in. I ended up locating the owner and I said, 'Listen, if this lot aren't out of this house by the morning, I'm coming back for you, mate.'

I told him what had been going on at the house he rented out and that evening he came there with me and asked, 'Will you come in?'

I kicked the door in for him, secured all the doors with new locks, and we got rid of the troublemakers. We found out where they were and told them to keep away from the street, 'or else'.

I went back about a week later and all the people in the street were happy and asked, 'What do we owe you?'

I replied, 'I want nothing off you, you're all right. Don't worry about it.'

They have had no trouble since. What the police, an MP and the local paper were unable to do, I had done in a matter of hours.

About six years ago, my brother, Peter, was driving me through the north side of Middlesbrough one afternoon because I'd had my licence taken away. I could see this car in front of us, swerving on the road and I said, 'He's pissed, him. Keep back from him, Peter, because he's going to hit you.'

The driver was swerving, going up and down grass verges, and stopping and starting again.

I said, 'What the fuck's wrong with him?

We came to a place called Gypsy Lane. It was about a quarter to four and there were a lot of kids walking home from school.

I said, 'Fucking hell, if he goes along this bank, he's going to kill these kids!'

There was little time to do anything, so I said to Peter, 'Get alongside this fucker because I'm going to get into the car.'

My brother said, 'No, you won't! You'll get yourself killed, Brian, you can't!'

Fortunately, the car in front came to a standstill and I jumped out of our car, ran and grabbed hold of the drunkard's car door. No sooner had I opened the door than he started driving away, so I dived in as far as my body would allow me and pinned the man down. I pulled the hand brake on, turned the ignition off and the car skidded across the road and stopped. I went to grab him and give him a bat. You fucking dickhead! I thought.

When I looked at him, I could see something was wrong, but he wasn't pissed! I smelled his breath and realised he had insulin deficiency. Then, while I was looking for his ID in the glove box, I saw the needles and other stuff diabetics use. I phoned an ambulance and they came and took him. His heart was going 1,000 mph and they said, 'You've probably saved his life here.'

There was the poor sod nearly dead and I was going to batter him! And you know, I never received a pat on the back or a commendation for doing that. Anyone else and they would have received a letter of recognition, but it was me we're talking about.

The man in the garden: this is a funny story. I was coming home with my mum and my dad, going through Thornaby, and on the left were these little bungalows where old people live. As we drove past, I caught a glimpse of an old man laid out flat on the path, face down with his arms stretched out.

'He's having a heart attack,' I said. 'Turn around!'

I was trying to remember my first aid and what you do. Sixteen compressions or ten compressions and then two breaths? Anyway, I jumped out of the car, vaulted over his privet hedge, it was about three feet high, and ran towards him. Fucking, bloody hell, he was lying on his belly with his hand outstretched; he had a brush and he was painting his step, and just his hand was moving! Imagine if I had flipped him over on to his front and started giving him a cardiac massage!

I felt about one inch tall. I sneaked back out and the man in the next garden asked, 'What's the matter?'

When I explained that I'd thought his neighbour was having a heart attack, he started laughing and agreed, 'Well, it does look like it from where you were standing!'

This is another one. These girls of the night, prostitutes, phoned me – not that I have anything to do with them. Anyway, they phoned me as a last resort. The girls were on the game down in Middlesbrough and there was a lad called Jermaine, a mixed-race kid, and every time they were making money or scoring drugs, because obviously he was on crack cocaine, he would beat them up – and I mean beat them up! He had broken one lass's arm and another lass's ribs. He wasn't their pimp, he was just robbing them. Taxing them. But there is taxing and there is taxing. He was the scum of the earth.

One of the girls said, 'He's knocked a girl over.'

He had broken her ribs, her arm and her two hips; knocked her over in his car just for a £20 score of crack. As soon as the girls get their crack, they stash it down their knickers, so the police can't find it. This fiend was ripping the knickers off them, taking the drugs, beating them and kicking them all over.

I said, 'When do we get this little bastard?'

We hid out of the way and watched out for him. One of the girls gave us the nod and he was dragged into the car. My mate put a blade to his eye and said, 'I'm going to pop your eye out, you little bastard!'

The arrogant cunt said, 'I'm going to get the police, I'll get the police.'

These types of people are good at giving it but when it comes to taking it they want to go to the police. Anyway, that was the end of him. We kicked the living daylights out of him and, after that, no more girls were beaten up. They were all over the moon.

I never asked for payment. When I see somebody bashed like that, especially girls, I just feel sorry for them. I know some of them are on the game and they shouldn't do this and that, but some people get led down the wrong path. They get hooked on drugs and then there is no way out.

While I was in prison, a man came to see me. His name was

Chino and he has passed away now, God rest his soul. He brought his son, Gino, with him. Chino told me of this man in Redcar – I won't say his name but he had four pubs and two nightclubs in the town – who owed big money to some lads. I think he owed 20 or 30 grand, something ridiculous like that, and they wanted the money straight away.

Chino put a proposal to me: 'Could you put your name forward and say he is working with you.'

So I phoned these people from prison and said, 'Can you leave him alone and he'll give you an extra five grand, and can he pay it over the year?'

I called Chino and said, 'A friend of yours will say that they will call it off, but these people are wanting to take him away and do him in or take the clubs off him.'

Chino said, 'He said to tell you that, when you come out, he'll look after you and will give you all the doors and the doormen.'

I said, 'Tell him I'm not really interested in the doors.'

News came back to me that the man I had pulled out of the shit said he would give me a weekly wage of so many hundred pounds for security.

I said, 'That will do me. Give me a grand a month and that will be that. Put it all through the books and then it's all legal.'

When I got out, I went to Redcar and into the pub and the doorman said, 'You can't get in, you're barred out.'

I thought, They've got some fucking bottle barring me out! I talked to my mate Smiler, who worked there, and he said, 'I'm not stopping you going in, Brian, you're my mate.'

The two-faced owner had phoned the police. I thought, You fucking scumbag, when I was in jail it was all right to help you. He used my name without paying me any money and then he wanted to get out of paying me what he had promised.

I went to see him to find out when he was going to start paying me monthly. I had done my part: I had phoned the people for him and stopped them taking his four pubs and two nightclubs. He had borrowed the money to put into the clubs and he couldn't pay the people back and they wanted the money or the clubs.

I thought, He has got some bottle. I looked behind and saw about six or seven police cars, police dog sections and maybe ten armed police – not fucking walking about with their guns but standing there ready to use them.

I went into the next pub he owned and there were policemen at that door. At every fucking pub and club he had, officers were standing outside with police cars nearby. One of the lads was listening on a scanner and he phoned me and gave me a running commentary, saying, 'They're watching you, because they're saying that they can see you.'

They have got CCTV cameras all over the High Street in Redcar. The lad listening to his scanner continued, 'The police are coming back and saying, "He is walking up to the next pub. Can we have all units to the next pub, all available units?" One on the dog section has said he's finished, but the senior officer has said to him, "You are not fucking finished until he has fucking gone home, you're staying on."'

This type of people, when they are in trouble they want help, but when it comes to paying they run to the police.

I had just got out of jail and was still on a licence, so I couldn't fart without the coppers knowing about it. I had to keep the peace, so I just fucked off and I thought, The fucking scumbag. But obviously I would never help the bastard again; next time I would tell his creditors to take him away and do him. This is the kind of people that you sometimes have to deal with and then they say, 'Brian Cockerill is trying to tax me.'

18 THE TAX MAN'S GUIDE TO TAXING

THE ONLY DEFINITIVE guide to taxing is what the Chancellor of the Exchequer says in his Budget Day speech. The Brian Cockerill guide to taxation is slightly different.

You could bump into somebody in the street and they could have drugs on them, or money. Say they are drug dealers and you take their drugs off them, it's very hard for them to go to the police. They can't just say, 'Mr Policeman, I've just had drugs taken off me.'

Mind, this has happened to me, but only once. You may recall I told you about the lad who was stuck between a rock and a hard place – face his supplier or go to the police and make a statement against me.

Dealers cannot just do that, because they shouldn't have the drugs in the first place. The best way around it, to make the biggest money, is to get at somebody in their camp, someone who is weak. There might be four drug dealers working, or fag people bringing cigarettes in, and you get the weakest one.

Say they are making ten grand a week, or they might get 30

229

grand of stock delivered or 20 grand's worth of stock or 20 grand in cash. You get them to tell you what day the delivery or hand-over is going to be and then you turn up and you take it off all of them, and maybe even slap the lad who has set it up for you, so as to make it look good.

Afterwards, he gets a good drink out of it for having taken a few slaps, and he gets his money back. You would make maybe 40 grand and give him ten, or you might give him a five-grand drink and give him his ten grand back. Or you might just go to a house, kick the door down, have them over and tax them that way.

Information of this sort mainly comes by word of mouth. People tell you he is doing this or she is doing that. You see, most of them cannot keep their traps shut. They strut around with their chests puffed out, bragging, 'I'm making ten grand a week' or 'I'm making 20 grand a week,' and they talk a load of shite.

They might make five grand and say they are making 20, but whatever it is nearly all of them stash their cash in somebody's house that they know, because you can't put it into the bank. The Tax Man's job is to instil fear into them in order to learn where they have stashed it.

An interesting story about money, told about the late Viv Graham by his father, Jack, says it all: 'I said to Viv, "You're crackers, man, put it away, salt it away." I used to say, "Have you ever heard about the grasshopper and the squirrel?" Viv would say, "No, what's that, father?" "The squirrel gathers all the nuts and it hides them all over. Now the grasshopper, he just jumps about and enjoys itself. The winter comes, the grasshopper has got nowt to eat, but the squirrel's got all its nuts to eat. You're not going to be 30 all your life; you're going to get to 40, 50 and 60. You can't keep this game up at that age." He would say, "Aye, man, father, I'm not bothered about when I get to that age, I'm living now, man."'

Viv was a grasshopper, but I am pleased to say that the common wholesale drug dealer is a squirrel. Give them enough fear and they will tell you where their stash is.

It was so easy. You would send a young lad, about 18 or 19, to their door and get him to ask if they've got a bit of gear. That is the door open and you are in, and you grab them. You just keep them there until you get the money and the gear, but in those days they used to have the money and the gear in all the same house; it was only because of me that they started splitting them up.

There have been occasions when I have had to use a hammer to hit them over the head or to break their hands, toes or kneecaps. My favourite game with them was the Little Piggy game.

They would ask, 'What's the Little Piggy game?'

I would say, 'Oh, you haven't heard of the Little Piggy game! Well, this little piggy went to market,' and then you would whack them over the toe with the hammer and by the second little piggy they would usually tell you everything.

Some of them aren't really bad; you do get some half-decent lads who are selling a bit of gear. But some of them are horrible bastards and you don't mind braying them. Some of them are horrible cunts and are working for the police as well as selling drugs. These scumbags will sell gear to anybody and are just vermin. I would say seven out of ten dealers are scumbags.

A bobby once said to this dealer, grinning, 'I love that Brian Cockerill. You make all your fucking money, sell all your drugs and he comes round and just takes it all off you.'

One of the lads from Hartlepool told me, 'It is like an honour for you to tax them, it is like, "I've been taxed by Brian" or "Well, he taxed me first" and "Yes, but he only took 10 off you and he took 12 off me."'

They used to have arguments like that in pubs and clubs.

There have been people who have got someone to have a go

with me but they have all failed and I have beaten them, and then I have gone back and taken more money off them because of that.

Nowadays, you might tax someone and take 30, 40 grand off them, where years ago you might have taken three grand and shared it between three people and then be out raving and taking ecstasy and coke.

Some people come to you and say, 'They are bringing 100 grand's worth of fags in.'

I tell them, 'I want ten grand to give you protection.'

Now I'm wiser, running about and doing things that are more sensible. You don't waste as much money. Years ago, I used to go out and there would be hangers-on. You don't get as many hangers-on when you are older because you recognise them for what they are, especially when you've been to jail.

When I got out, there were only a few people who would give me a drink. I mean, one lad would give me £200 and another one the same. The ones that were hangers-on, you don't see them but when you start making money again you are back up the tree and doing things and that is when you see them again.

When you are younger, you are more gullible, like Lee Duffy was. They would say, 'I'm your friend, Lee,' and they are bound to be your friend when you are sharing everything or giving them 20 or 30 ecstasy every night. You know who your true friends are when you are on your arse and you have got nothing and you are struggling or if you are in jail and you get a letter off someone and they have sent you a £50 postal order or a £10 postal order; still thinking about Brian. They are your friends.

Recently I got a phone call in the early hours and a lad said, 'I've got trouble with such and such.'

I said, 'I'm not coming out of the house at half-past two in the morning, especially when I don't get paid.'

The same lad, when I went to jail, never came up and never

gave my missus any money; he never came up and dropped me a few quid. I thought, Fuck you, I don't do favours now, I want paying. Favours don't pay your gas and electric bills, mate!

What it is now, there is less money to tax because there are that many dealers, especially with that Euro train tunnel opening up. There are so many people bringing drugs through. These mules have only got to hold the drugs inside them for four hours. The people are just swallowing so much gear now and there are so many drugs. I mean, every street has got a dealer; nearly every fucking street has got a peddler or somebody that takes drugs.

You might have had four big dealers in Middlesbrough, three or four in Hartlepool and three or four in Redcar. Every town would have three to five big dealers and then they would have a few people working for them, maybe only half a dozen. These days there would be 150 people working in Middlesbrough, 150 in Hartlepool, 150 in Redcar. There are just that many people selling drugs now.

Years ago, ecstasy tablets used to sell in the clubs for £20 each. Now they sell for £2! It's not worth it to tax them. If we had got caught with a thousand of them, we'd have been looking at ten years behind bars! All for £650 or something, so it is best to go for the fag men, they are the best for the money. But, like I say, I do security now and I get more money and it is legal.

When I was in full swing, the drug dealers used to pay me to keep me away. They would give me £100 or maybe £200. Even today there are a lot of dealers still saying, 'I work for Brian Cockerill.'

I have never even heard of them, they just say that because I am the biggest name in the area so they don't get their drugs taken off them and have a free hand selling the stuff. They say, 'Don't take them off him because they are Brian Cockerill's,' but they are not mine.

That is when the police think these boneheads are dealing for me. I can understand where the police are coming from, because, if they get a tip-off that a lad is supposed to be dealing for me, they actually believe it. That is why I have got the National Crime Squad following me about, but they never get anything because I have never got anything. My record speaks for itself.

I can talk to people, and people like me. They can sit down and tell me something and I will listen to both sides. I don't just listen to one side of the fence; I listen to both sides.

If someone has got a shop and they are getting burgled and robbed, I will go and see the culprits and say, 'Look, lads, whatever you are doing, do your business elsewhere and don't do it here because I'm looking after the shop now.' They will keep out of the shop when I say, 'I'll be coming for you. I don't want to fall out with you, but if I have to, I will.'

They keep out, they don't burgle and they go elsewhere. They are someone else's problem.

I have seen a change in the amount of people taking drugs compared with years ago. It is massive! I remember a survey on the telly not long ago where they were stopping people in the street and asking to put a patch on their heads to check if they were using drugs. Someone who is in the social services told me that 77 per cent of people stopped in the street were found with drugs in their system. That would mean there would be nearly 80 per cent fewer drivers on the road if you stopped all the drivers caught with drugs in their system, and it would probably bring the country to its knees.

On the same basis, it is likely there are more crackheads than we think walking around the street carrying out crimes. So I would say there is more call for my security services because of crack cocaine rather than heroin. People taking heroin usually fall asleep, but people who take crack just want another go, and another go, and another go, and you could spend £1,000 on it and still want another go. Crack gives an intensity of pleasure beyond the bounds of normal human comprehension, so it is highly addictive. People want another go so badly that they will do anything, and that is why there are so many prostitutes on the street now; it isn't the heroin, it is the crack. It is not physically addictive, it is mentally addictive! I mean, you can have a go at crack ten times in a row and your body doesn't crave for it. If you're on heroin, you need it to sustain you every day of your life, but crack is a mental thing. One go is too many, and 1,000 is not enough. And nowadays it involves just massive amounts of money.

If a shopkeeper was telling me, 'Brian, these crackheads keep causing trouble!' and those responsible didn't listen, they would get brayed, but they do listen. All I do is I go and see them. They all know me because they see my posters up in the shops, so sometimes I don't even have to go and see people.

A shopkeeper phoned me. Since using my services, she has had two incidents in six months. Before, it was two incidents a day!

I believe my future will take me to street security, charging people £1 a week to look after their house. I like to think that you are helping people. They would just need to put a cardboard cut-out of me at the end of the street to ward off any would-be burglars. They were doing that with police cars on motorways to curb speedsters, weren't they?

I like it when people come up to me, like that old woman when I cleared her street of louts. I feel great going home knowing I have done a good deed for the day.

19 STAYING TOP DOG

I'LL TELL YOU a story to show you what a top dog is all about. A problem was resolved when a dead landlord's brother hounded a girl renting a house. The guy had been killed abroad and his brother was on the make before his estate was settled.

His brother came to the girl and demanded, 'I want all the furniture!'

This is when the girl, who was in her early twenties, phoned me and pleaded, 'Brian, they're threatening me and there are four of them here!'

There was this lad and three of his mates, knobheads, and she was with her mum and her sister: there was Sharon, Tracy and her mum.

The guy left empty-handed, saying he would be back on Monday. He never turned up on Monday and then he phoned and said Tuesday. He never turned up on Tuesday either. Eventually he turned up to the house on the Friday and started threatening Sharon.

This is when she called me. I dashed round but they had gone by the time I got there. I thought, If he wants furniture, he can have furniture! I phoned a lad who owns a skip and I threw everything into it, three-piece suites, tellies, the fucking lot.

One lad asked, 'Can I have this?'

I said, 'Take what you want, mate.'

There were a couple of tellies and a DVD player and a video. I said to the girl, 'You can keep that for yourself and when he comes just give him my number and tell him that I, Brian Cockerill, took your furniture to the tip.'

What a load of fucking scumbags they are! They go around threatening women but when I come on the scene they don't want to know. A top dog doesn't have to attack those weaker than him.

In order to stay top dog, you have to train hard. What I do is train with weights six days a week. I do chest on a Monday and maybe one set of biceps, one set of 20, and then I will do legs the next day, squats, and then maybe biceps. On a Wednesday I will do triceps and biceps, on a Thursday I will do shoulders and then on a Friday I will do back, which is dead-lifting and pull-downs and things and then on the Saturday I will do triceps and biceps again, but strictly in sets of 20. And then I will box on a Monday; I will do four threes on the bag or box. On a Wednesday I will do one ten-minute round, just one round and nothing else, and also on a Saturday I might do the pad work. I might do six twos on the pads. Sometimes, though I'm not doing it now, I used to train twice a day and even three times a day. When I am training for an organised fight for money, I might drop down to 20 stone and then I would do 500 sit-ups.

When I was going to fight Lee Duffy or Garside or people like that, I would cut my body weight down because you couldn't go in at 23 stone unless you grabbed hold of them. If you are fighting someone who is a good boxer, like Garside, you know he, at 17 stone, is going to be faster than you, so you have got to come down nearer to his weight and at 20 stone you are still going to be more powerful.

You have got to have power. I started doing bag (boxing) work when Ernie Bewick said to me 12 years ago, 'Every fight is different, though, isn't it?'

I used to do just six twos or four threes all the time, but Ernie started me doing a ten-minute round. He would come down and watch me and he told me my right hand was excellent, one of the best for power he had ever seen. 'It's awesome!' he said.

If I hit anyone with that, it is goodnight to them, but you don't always hit your shots off, so sometimes you have got to have stamina. You might go on longer, you might have a fight with someone and beat them in three or four minutes and somebody else might jump in for a fight. But most fights are over in 20, 30 seconds and in one punch. You have got to remember, sometimes we go into a place with maybe 10 or 15 lads and you might have to fight one after the other.

Say you went somewhere like Manchester and they don't know you, or you go to Newcastle and sort out some trouble there, you cannot rest on your laurels. I can walk into Middlesbrough and there could be 50 lads offering you out. They might do some damage to me, but they will know I will be coming back to them and doing more damage, but years ago that didn't happen. You have to go through all that to become top dog.

Once you are there, then it is easier because your name carries you, your name is there before you. I can phone someone up and say, 'Listen, I don't want you in there tonight, blah, blah, blah,' and they won't go in, but pubs are a pain in the arse, that is why I don't do the doors.

I have benched 630 pounds and I have squatted just under 800 pounds for one rep. I am going to go for a world record attempt, which is somewhere near there, and I am going for 20 reps with

260 kilos. I have dead-lifted with six plates on each end for ten reps, but what I do is I split it up into three weeks. The first week I will do four sets of ten on the bench, four sets of ten, three sets of ten on the incline and three sets of ten and there would be medium weight and medium style.

The next day I would squat four sets of ten parallel squats, medium weights, medium style, and maybe four sets of ten with 600 pounds. I start off with three plates, I do 20 reps on the leg extension and then I jump on and do 380 pounds after my first set and I do ten reps and then I will do 400 pound, ten, then 500 pound, ten, then 600 pound, ten, and then maybe 650 pound for five sets.

Then I would do leg extensions. I do three sets of ten straight off with 50 kilos, one pause at the top and at the bottom. I will put the plates straight back on so you are doing 30 reps straight off but dropping the weights down slowly.

Then I will do the biceps, three sets of ten, but have a rest in between. I have 50 kilos on the stack and then put a few more plates on because the machine only goes up to 50 kilos. Arm muscles are just a small body group and you can afford to train your arms twice a week, because the smaller muscle repairs itself quicker, whereas the bigger muscles take longer.

The next day I would do shoulders, ten press for three sets of lateral raise and then I might do 20 or 30 reps on the pump machine. The next day I would do dead-lifts. I might do four sets of ten, five sets of ten with, maybe, six plates and go up to a medium weight.

Then I will do pull-downs on a long pulley or something, and then the next week would be what I would call my strict week, and it would be four sets of six, but super, super strict.

I will start with benching and when I bench I do four sets of six, but I will stop at the bottom and count one two, then press one and then come back down, one two, and then press two. I will do the full range of movements and just use the chest. I will just put the weights very, very lightly, but still so that it hurts, and do that through the week.

I will go on everything, like legs, all the way to the bottom and then back up. Then, the third week, I will train for power. You train only every three or four weeks for power, and that week I will start off doing eight reps on the bench, but increasing the weight and then I will decrease each set of reps, four, then two, one, and the same on legs and the same on everything else.

I still enjoy it, but sometimes you think, Oh, I've got to go to the gym, but if you see it as a chore you don't enjoy it. A fighter needs strong legs: they are like the foundations of a house. Weak foundations and the building will tumble down.

My best asset is my legs: they are like tree trunks, even though I was savagely attacked and nearly lost one. If you are five foot five and you put a stone on, you look good. But, when you are six foot plus, when you start training you put on a stone but you don't feel like you have put anything on.

You say to people, 'I've lost two stone.'

They say, 'Where?'

People are paranoid about their weight. I mean, I went to jail weighing 22 ½ stone and I came out weighing 18 ½. I had quite a few fights because people must have thought that the loss of weight would mean I wouldn't be able to fight as well. It doesn't quite work like that. They say it's not the size of the dog but the size of the fight in the dog. If you are a fighter, you fight, and that is it; you can be ten stone and still be a good fighter. But it still hurts to be hit by a 300-pound guy!

I keep myself in the condition that I am because I am always on the lookout for anything that could happen. I am always ready if anybody comes and is ready to have a go, but when I go out I am all right because people like me. I hardly get into fights, but I am always vigilant in case it happens. You stand in certain positions in pubs, or stand with the wall behind your back. I know it is an old cliche, but it is the best way. I could be talking to you, but I will be looking at everything else. I am not being rude, I am just looking because I can see things that normal people don't see.

I have been working on the doors for 20 years and you just see things, like certain lads in gangs, and can tell when they are going to cause trouble. I can suss certain people going in and I will see if that alarm bell in my head goes off. Or, later on, the club buzzer would go off and I would know it would be the one I sussed out going in. Nine times out of ten, I can tell you the lad who is going to cause trouble, just when he is walking in. It will usually be his cocky attitude. They are only idiots; there is no serious trouble, but they are going to get into trouble, maybe over somebody's wife or something. You can't say, 'You can't come in because I don't like the look of you.'

If I think they are going to cause trouble, I will say, 'Mind, any trouble and you'll be out tonight.'

I have advanced from that stage; I don't do that sort of work any more. I mean, these young lads are so drugged up that it would take a rhino punch to put them away. People still ask me to work on the doors all the time, but I am not going to go back to it. I can't be arsed with the doors.

A doorman could say, 'I work for Brian Cockerill.'

When a lad is full of drugs he could reply, 'Well, I don't give a fuck who he works for!'

They are full of cocaine, they are in and out of the fucking toilets all night long snorting coke, and people reading this book will be saying, 'He's right.'

Years ago, people would drink, but now they drink *and* they take drugs. I don't know what is going to happen in the next 20 years. Fucking hell, they might come in eating cakes or something like that. I bet the government will put a tax on drugs and they will become street-legal. There's big money to be made from it. You can be sure that someone in a high place will be putting things into place to bring that about.

I will be 41 years old this year, and I still feel like I'm 25. There's life in the old top dog yet! Remember, you have one life, but can die 1,000 deaths; you've got to live your own life, because you die your own death.